I0187945

# Sanctity

## The True Account of Vietnam Combat Veteran & Missouri State Investigator Tommy Ray Capps

### By Teresa Garrison-Capps

**Mozark Press**
**www.MozarkPress.com**

All rights reserved. This book may not be reproduced in whole or in part or transmitted in any form without written permission by the publisher, except by a reviewer who may quote brief passages in a review; nor may any part of this book be reproduced, stored in a retrieval system, or transmitted in any form or by any means electronic, mechanical, photocopying, recording, or other without written permission from the publisher.

Copyright © 2016 by Teresa Garrison-Capps and
        Tommy Capps

Published by Mozark Press, Sedalia, Missouri

Acknowledgement: Cover design and book layout by H.D. Ream

**DISCLAIMER:** *Statements or opinions expressed in the stories and articles of this publication are those of the author and do not necessarily represent the views or positions of any person or entity associated with publication of the book.*

ISBN: 978-0-9903270-4-2
Third Edition

# Dedication

We dedicate this book to our children and grandchildren and for all the generations to come. May the life of Tommy Ray Capps be an inspiration to all who read his story.

We also dedicate this book to our sons Corporal Andrew Christopher Capps, USMC, and Major Dustin Garrison Dunklee, JAG Army National Guard, who followed in their father's footsteps by serving our Country.

A special thanks and dedication to Jimmy Lee Capps for his contribution to his brother's memoir with childhood stories from his compilation entitled: *Brass Monkeys*, and to our sister Linda Fisher and her husband Harold Ream for their countless hours of advice and editing.

All proceeds from the sale of *Sanctity* will be divided equally and donated to the Morgan County Caring for Kids Coalition in the memory of our granddaughter Hope Ray Dunklee, and to the Veteran's Administration Nursing Home Facilities throughout Missouri in honor of our veteran fathers, J.C. Garrison, Army Air Corp WWII, and Robert Capps, Army WWII.

**PFC Tommy Ray Capps**

# Introduction

## "An eye for an eye makes the whole world blind." ~ Mahatma Gandhi

The Vietnam experiences of PFC Tommy R. Capps are factual, as are his childhood experiences. The names of the victims and the perpetrator of the case known as "The Dutch Country Rapes" have been changed to protect the innocent victims and to provide no publicity for the convicted rapist. This case is an actual event and the story herein is based upon actual events. We owe a special thanks to Brother Jimmy L. Capps for his contribution of childhood stories.

The "Letters Home" sections are written verbatim from the letters Tommy wrote to his parents while in Vietnam. The use of the phonetic spelling of words is not used to cast negative aspersions upon his lack of knowledge, but rather to prove that determination of self-improvement and continuing education at any age is possible and achievable. Also, Tommy stressed that his letters lacked the harsh reality of his life and death combat situations. He did not want to upset his parents and family members. As a combat infantryman, Tommy was ordered to destroy any letters he received from home to avoid the possibility of an enemy combatant contacting loved ones at home if he had been captured or killed.

Living with such a humble, honest man has always inspired me to become a better woman. Tommy also has taught me to slow down and appreciate each and every day and to be content with who we are and where we are. Anyone that meets Tommy is drawn to his unpretentious and genuine personality. I hope you, as a reader, are also inspired to treat others with respect and above all show love and compassion to those who no one loves.

*Teresa Garrison-Capps*

# SANCTITY

## A true account of
## Vietnam Combat Veteran PFC E-3 and
## Missouri State Investigator
## Tommy Ray Capps

Sanctity or the godliness of an entity or place;
Ultimately the choice becomes clear of
the **inviolable sanctity** of the human spirit.

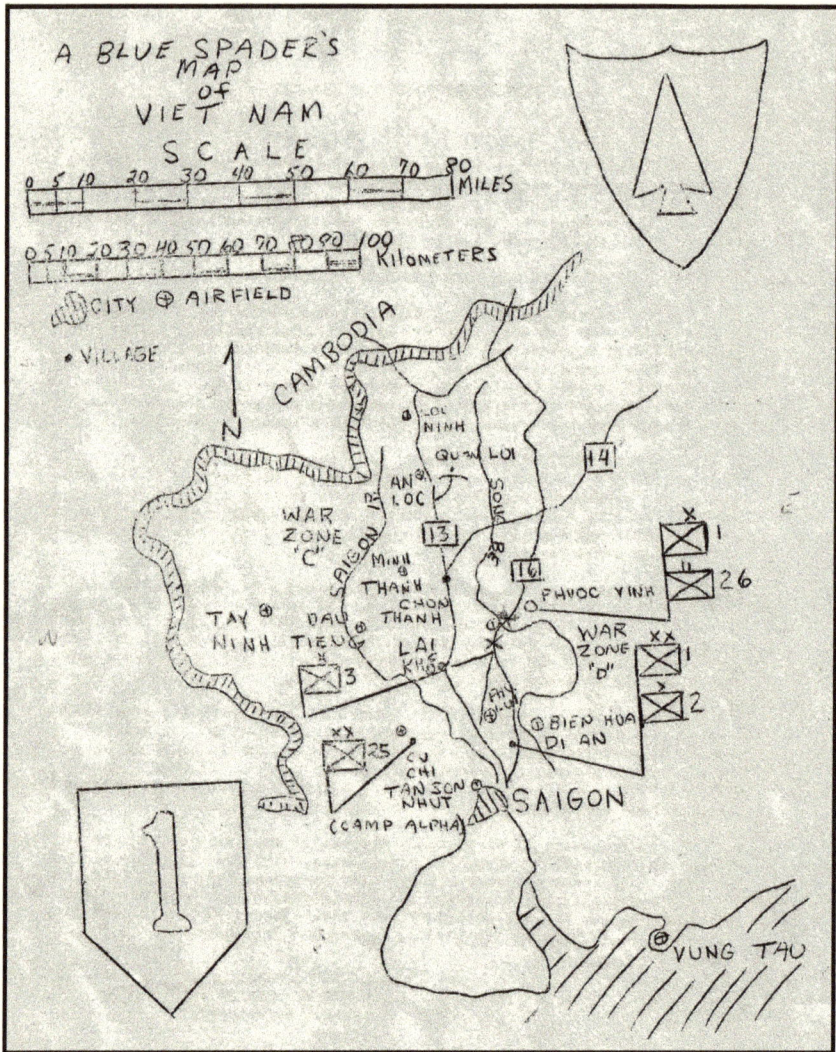

**Blue Spader Map**
**See page 168 for more information**

# Chapter One
# Field Stubble

Driving down the dusty gravel road, interspersed with the picture-perfect two story farm homes, fields of corn stubble and remnants of vegetable gardens, I couldn't help but think that it was great to be alive; not to say, that I haven't been happy to be alive all the other days since the 5th day of December 1966.

No, today was one of those exceptional, perfectly glorious, Missouri October days that made you want to stop time, breathe in the fresh sweet clean air and drink in the simplicity of just being alive. There was a hint of the coming chill in the air and a scattering of hoarfrost dotted the combined corn and soybean fields and clung to the wire fences enclosing each farms' property.

Some of the farms are deemed "Century" because as the name implies they have belonged to the same families for over one hundred years; however, most of the farms in Morgan County are now owned by the Mennonites. We all refer to them as Dutchy's and they refer to us, or anyone not Mennonite, as the English; no disrespect meant—just a marked distinction between the two groups. They are known to "plow deep" and feel a deep communion with the soil and their Creator. The Mennonites began their trek into Missouri during the 1960's. The remote small towns and cheap land soon became their promised land.

On this day, their fields, where in springtime were plowed and planted with iron-wheeled tractors and where throughout the summer months were rich with corn, soybeans and hay, now lay barren awaiting the long rest of winter. Their once abundant gardens would have been a desolate sight too had there not been the sprinkling of orange from pumpkins, green from peppers and red from tomatoes, left until the forecast of the first hard frost.

As I pulled my unmarked state car into the driveway of a Dutchy home, I pushed the button to lower my window, inhaled the fresh air and gazed transfixed on a field of crop stubble. Closing my eyes for a quick respite, the faint smell of evergreens permeated my nostrils and took me back in time. I sat frozen in the comfort of my car while my mind took me thousands of miles and years away from the sanctity of home. The helicopter, appearing now out of the east, was coming closer and closer and the increasing rhythmic "wop-wop" sound of the whirling blades found me in the peanut fields of Vietnam.

❖

October is also the month for change in South Vietnam with rainfall on the decline especially toward the end of the month as the region moves into its dry, hot summer months with an average temperature of eighty degrees. It was, however, *always* hot and humid. Our uniforms would rot off our bodies after just a week in the bush.

✦◈✦

Let me back up now and introduce this old soldier; I entered this world on October 19, 1946, in a small home in "Little Buffalo," an area in southern Morgan County, Missouri. My grandpa, or as we called him, "Poppy" Everett Whittle pulled my bornin' cry from me. I was the first-born son of Robert and Lula (Whittle) Capps. They named me Tommy Ray Capps, second child of what eventually would become a family of eight siblings. I grew up on a farm in "Birdsong Holler" that was about three quarters of a mile from the Lake of the Ozarks cove officially called West Proctor.

Although we were poor, I had the best childhood a boy could ask for. Times were tough during the latter part of the 1940's and 1950's and as we got older, my younger brother Jimmy and I were expected to pull our weight and do our share of the chores. I was proud to say, "My family never took no relief from the government like most of the neighboring families did." I think there are some lyrics to a country song that goes something like, "We were poor in money, but rich with love." Anyway, if there isn't, there ought to be.

At the age of nineteen, I had entered a foreign world. I reckon' I was as far from my home woods of Morgan County, as a person could get. I am not ashamed to admit that I was scared, and yet somehow I knew that my experiences here in Nam were going to impact the rest of my life.

I was on perimeter guard at the edge of a temporary base camp. Let me explain; my days in Vietnam as a member of the United States Army consisted of three occupations: ambush patrol, where every third night we were more or less on a suicide mission; listening post, where we were positioned in the bush about three hundred yards or more from the perimeter guard; and perimeter guard, the only place where I felt safe enough to get some rest.

You see, I was more or less cannon fodder for Uncle Sam—classic textbook picture of a high school dropout—draftee, who was sent to the front lines of combat with the 1st Infantry, 26th Division, bequeathed with an MOS (Military Occupational Specialties) of 11B10 (Light Weapons Infantryman). 11B or 11Bravo was also referred to as straight-leg infantry, or ground-pounders, or grunts. My unit was called "Blue Spaders" with the Big Red One. This particular temporary base camp was built on a knoll in the middle of a terraced peanut field, giving us a clear field of fire from any direction.

The peanut field loomed large in front of a line of trees marking the beginnings of the jungle. Perimeter guards were positioned in a circle surrounding the base camp. It was a series of foxholes or "graves" as we called them with machine gunners stationed at twelve, three, six, and nine o'clock. Mortar platoons set up sporadically behind the perimeter guards and would periodically fire off a mortar into the jungle, just to keep the enemy on their toes. The remainder of the perimeter was covered by riflemen, of whom I was one on this particular day.

All was calm and most of the gunners were kicked back and half asleep, when nature called. I handed the gunner on my right my M-16 and he gave me his pistol, which was a .45. All machine gunners and officers carried a .45.

I warned him, "Keep close watch, as I really don't want to die taking a shit."

He sat nonchalantly with his feet up, smoking a cigarette looking very unconcerned, but acknowledged my request with a quick, "Sure." His eyes drooped shut, but he still puffed on the cigarette hanging limp from his lips as I turned out onto the open field. It is a simple matter of fact that everyone poops and modesty was the first virtue you lost in war.

I quickly trotted out into the field of fire, and trying not to openly display my ass, went over the first terrace, unbuckled my belt, dropped my britches and squatted amidst the peanut crop stubble.

Let me stop here and enlighten you that *no one* and I mean *absolutely no one* with one week of experience on ambush patrol wore underwear. Underwear was a major source of chapping. And I guarantee that any gun-toting soldier with a chapped butt becomes one mean *SOB*.

Hunkered down, I heard a noise that sounded like paper rattling—a far off sound rushing through the dry, dead crop heads that quickly advanced toward *me*. Instantly I heard the gunshot.

When the bullet hit the ground, I knew exactly who had me in his sights. Another bullet whizzed by and then another as I lunged and groped the ground like a snake in a wagon track until I could finally heave myself into the foxhole. I didn't even bother to pull my pants up. I had one hand on the .45 and the other grasping a wad of my britches. I made a record-breaking fifty-yard dash with my pants down.

By this time, the gunner had opened up on the jungle in the direction of the gunshot. It was beyond me how quickly he came out of his sleepy stupor and opened up on the jungle with the sound of that first gunshot. Gunner's bullets came within forty feet of me, which he found a strange humor in.

With a crooked grin, he glanced my way and shouted, "You almost got your ass shot off, Cappy."

I knew I could never live it down if I returned home with gunshot wounds in my buttocks. My Ol' Man and brothers would have laughed me right out of Morgan County. All hell broke loose and the entire camp of trigger happy, snot-nosed, boy soldiers let the bullets fly. Even the gunners on the other side of the camp, opened up with crossfire.

We never found a body in the bush, so the sniper must have popped up and then high-tailed it back into the jungle as fast as I scrambled bare-assed back to the base perimeter. It is an eerie feeling to know you were in the sights of an enemy soldier targeting to kill you like a deer during huntin' season. But, at that moment in time, and on that October day in Vietnam, I was just happy to be alive.

⊷⊰⧩⊱⊶

I snapped back into my present reality as the Missouri State Highway Patrol (MSHP) chopper circled overhead. The men on board were on a mission to spot any evidence of a hiding spot or tracks from a person or a vehicle that could be discerned from their vantage point. We were in the thick of Mennonite country and the morning brought out the horses and buggies as these quaint folk prepared crops for the local produce auction.

"What a mundane life," I mumbled to myself.

I was startled as Max, another state investigator, walked up on my blind side, and asked, "What you lookin' at Capps?"

I replied, "Those Mennonite women are sure hard workers, aren't they?" Of course, in my recollection, *no one* has or ever will work as hard as my Poppy Whittle. He would walk nine miles to work—load railroad ties, which were balanced on his shoulders into railway cars, walk nine miles back home and then do the farm chores. I quickly echoed my thoughts aloud answering my own question, "Although no one has or ever will, work as hard as my Poppy Whittle."

Max and I could see several of the spic and span farm homes from our vantage point. All the clotheslines were being quickly, neatly and orderly filled with blue jeans on one line, white shirts on another and long dresses on yet another.

The Mennonite children were typically on their bicycles heading up the road to attend one of their many parochial schools in the area, but this morning all the picturesque refuge of the Mennonite community was gone. The men were hitching up their buggies and escorting their children to school.

Max began snapping pictures of the surroundings and the home. Max had been a forensic photographer in Kansas City and had retired to the country to finish up a career in law enforcement with Missouri's State Technical Assistance Team.

The agency we work for, also known as STAT, is comprised of specialized investigators with expertise in heinous abuse, deaths and sexual crimes against children. I was specifically trained to interview children and their perpetrators. We work at the request of law enforcement agencies throughout the state of Missouri who don't have the capability or man power to thoroughly investigate these types of crimes. We are also requested when a conflict arises, such as when a high profile citizen is accused.

Clearly, Max didn't understand the "simple ways" and definitely did not know the rules of Dutchy picture taking. With the stealth of a cat, a man came out of nowhere and stuck his hand in front of the lens of Max's state procured camera.

"We do not allow photography," he stated in their quintessential sing-song dialect that always sounded as if they were ending a sentence with a question.

I could tell he was a bit agitated, so I motioned for Max to let me handle the situation. With a calm demeanor, I explained, "We will respect your wishes, but we are here to find and stop the person violating your children and to prevent other innocent girls from being abused in their beds. Your homes should be a safe and secure haven, not a place where your children fear to close their eyes."

Let me make one thing clear about the Mennonites—they are not Amish. They adhere to the teachings of Menno Simons, the founder of the Mennonite movement during the Reformation. Menno Simons was educated for the priesthood in the Roman Catholic Church and must have been a very charismatic leader because when he renounced his church and priesthood, he had no trouble in extending his ideas and finding others to join his movement. Menno Simons differed with his superiors on church policies and established a "new order" of worship, and a set of rules or *Book of Discipline* for the conduct of those who followed his teachings.

Menno Simons' followers, popularly called Mennonites, were largely zealous persons of religious conviction to be found in Switzerland, Germany and along the Rhine down into Holland. Most of them were German-spoken; some were Holland Dutch. Both English and Pennsylvania "Dutch," so-called by the English in lieu of "Deutsch" are the languages of their homes.

All Dutchies are therefore bi-lingual, which consequently affords them a great advantage. The Missouri Order doesn't teach their children much of the English language until they reach school age, keeping them shielded from worldly evils or associating with any outsiders. Today, there are different sects within our Morgan County communities—from horse and buggy only, to driving a car.

But then again, there are different sects of car driving Dutchies. When the less conservative Mennonites began driving cars they would only buy black cars and paint all the chromed accessories and bumpers black. Thus, the locals called them "The

Black Bumper Dutchies." I don't know where that came from, but I assume there must be something in the Bible about shiny bumpers.

I'm sorry; I work on it daily, but for now I just find it hard to possess a blind faith in a God that allows for so much profane viciousness against innocent children. As my Ol' Man would say, "You can live like a Christian and still not believe in God." I do know that there are two places where a man will always seek out God: "War and jail."

In this case, because of the sensitivity of the circumstances, the Morgan County sheriff's office personally requested that I lead this investigation. Prior to STAT, I was the Morgan County sheriff's detective and they knew my passion for "finding the bad guy" was a "force to be reckoned with."

The crimes that occurred in Morgan County during a four-month serial event were not disclosed by the Mennonite community until this most recent sexual assault was reported by the Mennonite elders to local law enforcement. The closed Mennonite communities don't want to involve themselves in the laws of the English. I am told that they don't want to stand in judgment of another human being—their whole society is based upon pacifism and forgiveness. They proclaim, "It's God's will," as they speak in their sing-song dialect.

I have become calloused by my thirty plus years in the "business," and I have seen it all! The only sanctity in my world is the fact that I was instrumental in the conviction and imprisonment of over 235 pedophiles and child murderers in the state of Missouri.

I often wondered if I could get by with punching a bad guy in the nose, or worse, if I concluded it with the phrase, "It's God's will"—or blame it on PTSD. I have often questioned why I didn't return home from Vietnam in 1966 with PTSD. Could be, as I have often explained to my wife, that either I have a better handle on life and death and all the atrocities in-between, or I am just too shallow brained.

**Poppy Whittle with his mules**

# LETTERS HOME

Sept 7 66<br>8:30 p.m.

Hi Mom

Well I got here just fine. We will probly leave here sometime tomorrow but not sure. I just wrote Sally a letter and I am so down in the dumps I can't even think to write but I figure I had better drop a line to let you all know that I'm just fine and that I have already prosscess through and will be leaving hear as soon as we get transpertion. I'll send my address as soon as I get one and that should be before the weekend anyway but who knows.

Well Mom I got to quit now tell everyone Hi for me and take care of dad
Besure to tell Sonny Hi also grandma and granpa Whittle and Capps.

See you soon (364 days) at least

Pvt Tom
US 55841739

**Grandma Alpha & Grandpa Everett Whittle
on their wedding day
November 15, 1913**

## Chapter Two
## Common Sense

Max and I sat down at the kitchen table of the Zuckholder's with our notepads, tape recorder and pamphlets sprawled across the length. I always take a mental picture of my surroundings during an investigation, and today was no different except, there is nothing on the walls. The only notable pieces of furniture are a couch, rocking chair and a grandfather clock standing in one corner. Mrs. Zuckholder must have meant a lot to her husband, you see, Mennonites don't buy engagement rings—they buy their betrothed a clock.

The noticeable absence of pictures reinforces their beliefs in the non-importance of self, not that they don't hold their family in highest esteem. They live a simple life, void of all the vain and worldly distractions of this corrupt planet. Evidently, they value quiet and an uncluttered mind more than I do or anyone else out in the English world for that matter. As the old saying goes, "Ignorance is bliss." I beg to differ with that conjecture.

I do know that I could never live without my satellite TV, iPhone or Internet. In this day and age, I don't know how anyone functions without the modern conveniences. I have often compared my brain to a TV when people ask how I can do the job I have. I tell them that I merely change the channel in my mind or completely turn it off. Otherwise, the sheer deviant violence can consume you and devour your soul. But like I've implied before, I am calloused to the core.

It was September 7, 1966. I was nineteen years old the day I landed in Vietnam at the Saigon International Airport with a bunch of other naïve, green-horned, bald-headed, soldier boys. I was your typical 1966 draftee; a high school dropout with the lucky lottery number of 31. I knew I would be going to Vietnam since my Ol' Man served in WWII and the Capps' lineage of service could be traced back as far as the Revolutionary War.

My, too numerous to count, great-grandfather, William Hurst, in the month of July 1780, entered into the service of the United States as a volunteer in a corps of horsemen in a company commanded by William Campbell, in a regiment commanded by Colonel Archibald Lochry. He furnished his own horse and equipment at his expense.

He fought in the battle called "Lochry's Defeat" and as the story was written, was taken prisoner by Mohawk Chief Thayandanagea who wore the scarlet red British uniform with epaulets. Most of the 400 that Hurst rode with were killed by the "redskins." My grandfather William Hurst was taken prisoner and held in Detroit. From there he was moved to Montreal, where he remained a prisoner of war until he was exchanged and sent home to the United States. He landed in New York City around Christmas 1781. We know all this to be true, because in 1832 Congress passed a bill authorizing payment of pensions to Revolutionary War veterans, and William Hurst was required to submit a sworn affidavit committing his service to pen when he filed for this pension and was awarded Pension No. S. 31155.

Additionally, my great-great-grandfather Cpt. Jacob Capps fought for the Union at the Battle of Tuscumbia, Miller County, alongside my great-great-uncle Lieutenant Silas Capps during the Civil War. Service to our country runs deep within my bloodline. Jacob Capps, William Quick, William Graybeal, Peter J. Whittle, Solomon Keeth and John H. McGowin all served on one side or the other during the Civil War.

So you see, I knew I had no choice but to serve, and besides I wouldn't have dreamed of "burning my draft card" or "dodging the draft." I knew the significance of the word coward, and I was proud and determined to carry on the family tradition.

I was raised in the backwoods of Missouri, in an area known as Ivy Bend, although many of my close relatives call it Broken Circle, refusing to admit where their roots actually lie. It was a remote, rough wooded area, where few lived and no outsider wanted to be after dark. My momma, Lula Ellen Whittle, was born in 1927, the daughter of hard-working prairie land farmers, and with my father, Robert Capps, they were raising their family in this godforsaken, isolated and remote place. But to me, it was heaven on earth!

Momma always told anyone that would listen, that if the Capps' could sell rocks they would be millionaires; they had an over abundant supply. Her father-in-law and my grandpa Charlie Capps claimed that the Republicans stole all the dirt and moved it to Illinois right after the Civil War. "The Reconstruction Period," Grandpa Charlie called it. "And that is why Illinois is flat and Missouri is covered with rocks."

Grandpa Charlie and the Ol' Man bought many acres of the wild Ozark land when it still bordered the Osage River, soon to be consumed by the Union Electric Company of St. Louis in the development of the Lake of the Ozarks, or as my relatives called it, "that damn dam and worthless lake." Charlie's father,

Lindsey Capps lived and died on a houseboat tethered in the Osage River. Grandpa Charlie lived in a houseboat he found floating down the lake. He pulled it up onto a hillside and built a foundation around it. He was quite the hillbilly philosopher, one of his favorite quotes often repeated was, "The world went to hell, when people started shittin' inside and eatin' outside."

**Grandpa Charlie's houseboat**

We didn't have electricity until 1953 and now in 1966, my parents still didn't have a phone. I grew up in a home without running water, indoor toilet or electricity. My momma gave birth to a new Capps every couple of years and had to haul water from the spring for cleaning, drinking and bathing. Many a day I helped my momma with the laundry, hand washing worn out diapers and hand-me-down jeans, which we hung on tree limbs and low growing bushes to dry. I vividly remember running the rocky Ozark hills barefoot from May until September when I and all of my brothers and sisters got a new pair of shoes for the school year. We didn't even get underwear until we went to high school.

Momma and the Ol' Man

Momma fretted and worried constantly—only consolation was that her children were always well fed. We dined on squirrel, fish and lots of pork from the hogs we raised. Having grown up during the depression, Momma was just grateful that her children would never know the pain of hunger. Although illegal, the Ol' Man sold catfish for the other necessities of life.

Did you know that a hog will eat catfish? Maybe

Grandpa Charlie's hog farm

that is why our hogs tasted so good. There is an ol' Capps' family tale, which has probably been exaggerated over the years, but it goes something like this: Grandpa Charlie Capps went fishing about every day. As he came back into the cove, the pigs would swim out to meet his boat. He always gave them the chum

**Grandpa Charlie's hog farm**

fish—drum, gar and after skinning—the delicacy of catfish innards. Some folks say that a pig can't swim, because they would cut their own throats with their dew claw, but the Capps family begs to differ.

Jimmy, my brother who was two years younger than me, was my best friend and cohort in everyday adventures. We agreed on most of the important things in life, *especially fishin'*—by far the very best way to spend a day! Don't get me wrong now, swingin' on grapevines, huntin' squirrel, chasin' lightnin' bugs and stealin' tomatoes from Uncle Sid's garden were great activities too for two young boys, but fishin' was by far, the best entertainment on the face of the earth. It was a wonderful childhood, except for the occasional whippin', which were well deserved, from the Ol' Man. One thing about it, we all grew up to be hard working, respectable adults.

It was rumored that the Pendergast family in Kansas City, with its Mob ties, often dumped bodies deep in the woods and lake of my childhood. As I have emphasized, Ivy Bend was and remains a remote, yet beautiful, densely wooded sanctuary. Even today it is a foreboding place to live as drug addicts and other criminals find it an excellent place to live off the grid.

Besides fishing, Jimmy and I spent many hours huntin' in the dense forests of oaks, piss elms, dogwoods, redbuds and cedars. Why, I could make a head shot on a squirrel from twenty-five yards with an open-sighted 22 rifle. Guess that skill earned me the MOS of 11B10. I was just a backwoods "ignert hillbilly"; deep down I knew I had an advantage over some of these educated, city boy soldiers.

◆──◈──◆

The sergeant in charge divided us up and led us to buses reinforced with heavy screen over the windows to keep hand grenades from being thrown into the bus. As we boarded, they issued each of us an M-14 rifle and ammunition in case of attack. We drove out of the city toward a field camp.

Along the side of the road, much to our amazement, women, men and children would just squat and relieve themselves. I was sitting next to a black soldier from Texas. I didn't know any black folk; they didn't live where I grew up. We didn't even have any blacks in the schools I attended in Stover. They had to attend their own school in Sedalia. Hell fire, it was a known fact that there was a Stover city ordinance enforcing a no blacks allowed in Stover after sundown. We were, after all, south of the Mason-Dixon Line.

❖

Richard Stringer, the teenage son of the Ol' Man's hired help, taught us boys all about the black folks. Now Richard's parents, Frank and Linda were known squatters in the Ivy Bend, moving from one old deserted house to the other. As my Ol' Man said, "They didn't have a pot to piss in, or a window to throw it out of."

Frank was our Ol' Man's working partner and was one of those men who knew just about everything, and he liked to share his knowledge. He wore on most people's nerves. I suppose the Ol' Man mostly ignored him and just appreciated him for what he was, a hard worker.

One day Richard was over at our place and started talking politics, as most kids will do, imitating their parents. He asked what Party we belonged to— Democrat or Republican? My brother Jimmy asked him, "Which kind is the best?"

Richard said, "Democrats is the best."

Jimmy said, "How come?"

"Cause niggers is Republicans!" Richard explained.

We told Richard that we liked nigger toes, thinking of the chocolate covered crème candy the Ol' Man bought us every Christmas. Richard could see how ignorant we were on the subject so he explained how their skin was black as tar and it wouldn't come off. He said it was just like having walnut stain all over your body, only it never wears off. We were in a state of wonder because neither one of us had ever seen a black person before. Jimmy settled the dilemma and declared, "I reckon we must be Democrats, cause we shore ain't niggers." I have never been racist and don't ever intend to be one; this is just how isolated hillbillies thought.

I did experience racism first hand in Louisiana when I drove myself and my wife down to Ft. Polk for Advanced Infantry Training (AIT). It was then that I became aware of the evil of racism. Every gas station bathroom in Louisiana was for "Whites Only." I didn't even know what that meant.

I couldn't help but think how different my upbringing was from my Texas bus mate, but here we were together. I knew he would have my back, and I would do my best to make sure he got back to Texas. Strange, but no one gave a crap about the color of your skin in the middle of a war.

For some southern white boys, it was too much to share the same barracks with black boys. I witnessed a black recruit knock down every bunk in our barrack as he proceeded to teach the arrogant, racist white recruit that we all bleed red. It is my belief that if we are all created in God's image, then God must be every race and every gender.

I wasn't raised up by "church-goers," but I was taught to be non-judgmental. My Ol' Man stressed to us that everyone was equal and we were taught to consider others circumstances because we could find ourselves as outcasts just as easily. Looking down on others was not our way. Never has been and never will be.

◆━━◈━━◆

The Vietnamese road was pitted and corduroyed causing us to bounce and jostle one way and then the other. Our drab Army green bus was eerily quiet; just the occasional "ugh" as the ride got rough. No one said a word; we all just stared silently into our future. My mind kept wandering back to the past and the hills of Missouri. Silently I pondered, "God, I wish I was anywhere else, but here."

God's honest truth, my third day "in country," they marched us infantrymen way out onto a field of foot-tall grass, bordered by the jungle, to a set of bleachers. They sat us down facing the open field to give us an orientation and training on how to spot "land mines" as we patrolled the jungle. The "people in charge" had planted a bunch of duds—or so they thought. I was just a green hillbilly replacement grunt; however, the thought ran through my mind that this place is out in the boonies—what would prevent the Vietnamese from sneaking in here? Unfortunately, my intuition was spot on. Those shrewd little bastards had planted the real McCoy.

We were led out onto the field, when an ear-piercing explosion rocked the air. Someone yelled, "Incoming!" Another screamed, "Hit the ground!" Then a second and a third explosion followed.

Screams of the men without legs and feet echoed in my ears. Chaos ensued as most of the officers thought we were being mortared. Many of the boys newly turned soldiers were puking and some even crying. My upbringing of slaughtering pigs and deer somehow softened the bloody shock. This cruel initiation to the reality of their situation had just manifested itself in blood and human misery.

The sergeant started barking orders and told us to walk slowly, and follow in the footsteps of the soldier in front of us to avoid the three-pronged triggering devices, no bigger than a matchstick. It seemed like time stood still as we slowly, step by step, moved back toward the bleachers. As soon as we made it back to the safety of the bleachers with no further detonations, it was discovered that one of the injured soldier's M-16 rifle was left in the middle of the field. Another sergeant volunteered to walk back out to retrieve the gun and sure as shit, another land mine took off his feet. The military careers of four soldiers ended that day. It was a wonder that more of us didn't get "blown to hell" during that first day of jungle training.

They finally came to their senses and brought in an APV (Armored Personnel Vehicle) and tripped thirteen more live mines. To this day, I don't know how the United States of America ever won a war. I do take pride in saying, "We were winning when I was there!"

---

Kristin sobbed as she talked with her mother and father in broken English and Dutch. She had just turned eight years old, and now her virtue and faith in the human race had been destroyed in the darkness of one night. All of her siblings had been taken to the grandparent's home down the road to shield them from the harsh truth of what mankind is capable of. Ironically, the aroma of Mrs. Zuckholder's fresh baked bread filled my nostrils and flooded my memory of home and a less complicated childhood.

Kristin's mother held her on her lap, as her father Jacob Zuckholder explained to us, "I heard some thumps, coming from Kristin's room." He emphasized that Kristin shared her room with two younger sisters, but they had escaped any *"misbruik."*

The Mennonites, being such trustworthy and trusting folks, never locked their doors. This practice was going to soon change. I was told that the local farm and home store sold out of door locks.

Jacob continued, "I grabbed a flashlight, but didn't turn it on until I heard a noise in the back corner of the room. I shined the light over toward the noise and there huddled in a crouched position, was the outline of a person. I couldn't tell if it was male or female at the time. The figure was slight of stature, so I really couldn't determine if it might be one of my daughters. I startled the figure, he jumped up, lunged at me and knocked me on the floor. It was then that I recognized that this was a man. He then ran down the hall and down the steps and out the front door. By the time I could regain my wits about me, my wife was screaming and I ran to comfort her. When I made it out to the front porch, I could see nothing, and the only sound was the barking of dogs down the lane and across the field."

It is hard for me to understand why a man wouldn't run down the culprit and beat him unconscious. These men can build a barn in a day—they ride bicycles to town thirty-five plus miles roundtrip—but lift a finger in anger? No! If only the rest of the world could adhere to their peaceful way of life. They exemplify turning the other cheek.

Kristin's mother, Eva Ruth, was apprehensive when I asked her to tell me what she had seen. Women, in the Mennonite community are taught at an early age to be subservient and obedient to their husbands. She gave a pleading look toward her husband as if begging, "Please let me share what I remember." He gave her a scowl look and shook his head no.

Jacob then replied, "I told you what she witnessed."

"I know what you saw," Max snapped brusquely, "but we need it from her mouth." I directed a grimaced frown toward Max from across the table, and without saying a word he knew his sharp reprimand had offended the Zuckholders.

I have always had a disarming way about me, especially with the female of the species and was even known as the "Andy Griffith" of STAT. During my many years in law enforcement, I learned that you can usually obtain information without even asking a question if you use some common courtesy and tact. I had a country charm that could diffuse the tensest of situations. In fact, in my thirty years of law enforcement, I never once had to use my weapon. I treated people the way I wanted to be treated, after all, as my Poppy Whittle always said, "Us-ins all pull up our britches the same way, one leg at a time."

"Mr. Zuckholder," I began in a quiet non-authoritarian tone, "I believe that it would benefit your community if you allow us to interview your wife and daughter. But only with your permission...to insure that all your daughters are safe and to protect all of your kinsmen's daughters from this boy. We sure don't want this to continue, do we?"

Jacob looked Max right in the eyes and replied, "No, we don't, but I only want my family to talk to you." Max, rather indignantly stood up, and walked out the front door to the porch.

As the door opened with a grating screech, it dawned on me that no one could enter or leave without being heard. "Jacob," I asked, "can you hear the front door open when you're upstairs?"

He very hesitantly replied, "Why, yes, and I have been meaning to oil those hinges."

"Did you hear them last night?" I inquired.

"I don't recall, but then I am a sound sleeper."

Eva Ruth said something in Dutch to Jacob, then turned to me and said, "I heard them, but thought it was just the wind catching the screen door that was left unlatched by one of the children. I didn't think too much about the noise until now. The sounds from the bedroom woke both of us. When I heard the scuffling and thud, I jumped from our bed and ran to the bedroom door; that was when I encountered the figure, running past me. Our eyes met in the dim light and I screamed, 'I know those eyes'; *behoren voor de duivel!*" It doesn't take a translator to know she was talking about the devil.

Anyone familiar with the Mennonite community knows they are avid readers. They are by no means a backward society. Most end their formal education at the eighth grade, but today the elders are encouraging members to higher education for their teachers, computer technicians, doctors and psychologists. The progressive sects have acquired cell phones, computers and fax machines. Even some of the moderately conservative sects have telephones and electricity. They are an industrious people, and as I mentioned before, own most of the farmland and businesses within Morgan County.

The Mennonites never had a problem during the depression or the most recent recession and there is no such thing as unemployment in their communities. They are, by no means, *lazy*. I have heard some bigoted people complain that the U.S. is being taken over by the Mexican ethnicity; no my friends—it is the Mennonites, and I really don't have a problem with that.

⬥≫≪⬥

My momma spent almost thirty years, after her career raising youngins ended, managing a factory in Versailles. They made grass catchers for Sears and other brand lawnmowers, and she preferred hiring the Mennonites. They were always dependable and hard workers. They were also used to working in the heat because the old factory had no air conditioning. The Dutchy women told her that they gave their entire earnings to their family and Church. The irony of my momma's work career was that she did not get a retirement pension like the men in other states that held the exact same managerial position.

⬥≫≪⬥

The Zuckholders' were of the conservative sect—no phones, no cars and only electricity in the barn.

I asked Eva Ruth, "Do you think you could draw a likeness of the person? And do you think you and Kristin could write down exactly what happened?"

In my business, I had interviewed molested children as young as three years of age. I had earned the reputation of gaining the trust and confidence of child victims. For some reason, children found in me a trustworthy, caring soul and would disclose the darkest of their secrets. Even a perpetrator would shake my hand after I wheedled a confession out of him that would put him behind bars for years.

Truth be known, I was seething with rage and I could have gladly castrated and shoved his parts down his throat. One can only hope that they all receive some prison justice or justice at the pearly gates.

Like I was saying, I could talk a nun out of her habit. Back in the office one day, my supervisor was proudly bragging, "You won't be able to get my four-year-old daughter to go anywhere with you. We have taught her from an early age not to talk or go anywhere with strangers."

I challenged him to bring her to the office and time how long it would be before she would follow me to an empty room. I always wore cartoon neckties and most all children are intrigued with the brightly colored characters. It took less than five minutes, and I had convinced her to take hold of my tie and lead me to the empty office space. Her father was astonished, but given the fact that he was also in the office, it wasn't a very accurate experiment, but with this example, you can fully understand how easy it is to prey on the innocent.

⊷⟨⟩⟩⟩⟩⟩⟩⟩⟩⟩⟩⟩⟩⟩⟩⟩⟩⟩⟩⟩⟩⟩⟩⟩⟩⟩⟩

I usually videotaped my interviews with no one but me and the victim in the room, but here again the Dutchies don't want their pictures taken, and Kristin wanted her father to accompany her.

I knew Kristin should have gone to a hospital for possible DNA recovery, but her mother had already bathed her, washing away the evidence.

The Mennonites have their own clinics and now even their own psychologists within each community, and a trip to a hospital is sometimes a decision first presented to the elders. They have come a long way since the very conservative ones limited medical intervention believing their *Book of Order* that contends, "*...health is a gift from God and our bodies are temples of the Holy Spirit, we seek to be better stewards of our health. At the same time, because we are finite creatures and because we believe in the resurrection of the dead, we will accept limitations on medical intervention from the beginning through the end of life.*"

I also knew it was going to take a visit to the bishop if there was going to be justice for Kristin and the others.

**Grandpa Charlie and Grandma Rosa Capps**
**June 8, 1922, Linn Creek, Missouri**

# LETTERS HOME

16 Sept 1966

Hi Mom, well here I am in Viet Nam the other part of the world. The weather is great. It rains half the time. The other half its so hot you can't breathe.

How's Dad? Did he make the operation OK? How's the kids like school? Is Grandpa and Grandma still down to the house? How's Grandpa Capps? OK I hope. Is Mrs. and Mr. Wilson OK? I sure hope so. I would like for you to give her my address when you see her I mean then. It's getting dark and I'm going to have to close perty soon. Say Hi to everyone for me and you all take it easy.

Bye the way I'm living in a tent and I'm still waiting to go to my regular outfit which is on a mission now but there suspose to be getting back any time now. So I should leave tomorrow. I'm perty tired out tonight from all the work I've been doing. I'll be looking for a letter from you so write when you can and send Larry's address.

Well Mom I'm closing now. I'm just fine.

Your son
Tommy

P. S. give my address to Sonny if he's still at home if not send it to him.

PFC Tommy R Capps
US55841739
COB/BN 26 inf.
APO San Francisco Calif.
96345

**Great-Grandpa John McGowin**
**1914**

# Chapter Three
## Shangri-La

Life was a challenge for me, seeing as how I was the oldest male of four brothers and three sisters. From the early age of five, it seemed like I was always changing one or another of a baby brother's or sister's diapers. At the age of six, I would take my little brother Jimmy swimming and fishing down in an area unpopulated and secluded. Our momma was scared to death of the water and would have had a nervous breakdown if she had known we were swimming in the lake.

The local fishermen had piles of glass Purex bottles stored along the banks. These glass jugs had a carrying ring located on the neck. This ring was great for tying on to trotlines and they fit perfectly around a kid's finger. They became our flotation devices.

One hot summer day Jimmy decided to float out to the middle of the cove where he lost grip of the bottle ring. Instantly, to my relief, he popped his head back above the water and doggie-paddled back to the shore. That is how he learned to swim. We were only supposed to wade in the creek, but being mischievous daredevils, we pushed the envelope.

Today, my parents would have been charged with child neglect, but back in those days the older siblings were taught responsibility and I knew if anything ever happened under my watch, it would be the worse "lickin'" possible. Besides, our momma was busy takin' care of all the other babies. Women think they have a stressful life nowadays, but I guarantee it was nothing compared to how my momma had to raise us.

Remember, we had no electricity, no running water and no indoor toilets. The source of our water was a spring that was about a quarter of a mile from the house. It was a joyful day in 1954 when we could afford to dig a well at the homestead. Some of the original Amish that first came to Morgan County would buy a house and rip out the electricity and plumbing. I'm guessing they figured modern conveniences were the devil's handiwork. We considered it a blessing from heaven above.

Before WWII my Ol' Man worked with the CCC (Civilian Conservation Corps) until he was drafted for the duration. He recalled seeing the first jets flown by the Germans over France. Upon his return and the birth of my sister and me, he moved us to the state of Kansas where he helped build grain elevators. They moved back to Missouri when my momma threatened to leave him in the flatlands. He spent the rest of his life working in construction and raising hogs.

The term Ol' Man isn't used in disrespect, it was a family tradition. Our Ol' Man called his dad the Ol' Man; this term of endearment fell back four generations.

Jimmy and I, being the eldest sons, were in charge of taking care of the family's cash crop—"hogs." At five a.m., before daylight, we were awakened from our childhood dreams with a bellow equaling that of a drill sergeant, "Rise and shine, boys!" He never had to holler twice.

It was time to get outside and complete our morning chores. Hogs had to be fed and watered every morning and every evening, not to mention the numerous cold winter nights I spent trying to warm up baby pigs. I had to pull one hundred pound feed sacks out of the storage shed and drag them over to fill the feeders. Brother Jimmy was in charge of filling the two fifty-gallon water tanks for the "fattnin'" hogs, as well as the troughs for the sows with litters. We knew that we had just enough time to get all the chores done, get the awful smell of hog manure washed off, change into our school clothes, eat some cornflakes and get on the school bus.

I am positive that nothing about chores has ever changed in the Dutchy world, unlike the pampered generation of my children and grandchildren. Our Ol' Man, rest his soul, was hard as nails, and although at that time we resented having to work so hard, we admired him—yes, loved him.

Most of all I learned responsibility and the satisfaction only hard work produces. And above all, respect of my elders. If any of us boys ever talked back, we would have been "knocked into next year." Another lesson not forgotten—there is nothing meaner than a sow with piglets, unless it is a water buffalo, but I would not encounter them until my latter teenage years and a world away.

❦

Responsibility and dependability were two concepts that I understood *to-the-letter*. Before I was fourteen years old, I had saved the lives of three of my friends and one was my brother. My intentions are not to boast about being a hero, but standing by and doing nothing was not in my DNA.

Momma was heading down the Ivy Bend Road with a car load of kids. The only air conditioning of that era was having all the windows rolled down and there were certainly no seat belts. My brother Donnie was five years old, and I was twelve. I was sitting in the front seat next to the right-side window, and Donnie was standing in the backseat directly behind my right shoulder.

Suddenly a dog darted out of the woods and directly into our path. Mom swerved the car to the left and simultaneously slammed on the brakes. Donnie became a flying projectile. He sailed by my right shoulder—instinctively I grabbed Donnie's feet as he soared out the window. I held him off the ground until Mom got the car stopped.

I remember his eyes—the wide-eyed look of panic and fear. The pleading eyes crying for help. I would see those eyes throughout my life and career, those same eyes of fellow brothers in wartime, and then the eyes of abused children that seem to reach inside my very soul with their silent plea to be rescued.

The next life I saved was a friend and neighbor boy who couldn't swim. Jimmy and I were wading in the lake's shore at Wigwam Cove through a thicket of smartweed with a childhood friend, Raymond Webb.

Suddenly the shallow bank disappeared beneath Raymond's feet. He stepped out into the creek bed that was several feet deeper than his head, and disappeared beneath the water. I distinctly remember, to this very day, his eyes as he flailed helplessly above the water, appearing briefly before returning to the deep water. I went in after him.

We didn't know anything about resuscitation, so it was a blessing that after dragging him to the bank, he coughed and sputtered, choking up the lake water. We never told anyone! We didn't want to get banned from our lake explorations.

Jerry O'Neil was the third. I met Jerry the year I turned thirteen. His parents had a lake cabin in Luvin's subdivision where they spent summer weekends. His parents lived in Independence where his dad worked at Sheffield Steel. They brought their son Jerry, who was suffering from muscular dystrophy, to the lake at every opportunity.

Tommy's aluminum boat

Jerry's dad had custom built him a wide, flat-bottomed boat, equipped with a 10-horse power outboard motor and allowed him the independence to putter around in Luvin's Cove. When we first met, Jerry could still walk, and he still had some arm strength, but he was growing weaker each day. They didn't expect their son to live through his teens.

One summer afternoon, as luck would have it, or by pure providence, I came around the cove in my aluminum fishing boat handed down to me by the Ol' Man, just in time to witness Jerry struggling to get his boat motor started. After several unsuccessful pulls, he managed a pull that brought the motor to life in full throttle. The thrust jerked the boat, throwing Jerry into the water.

The boat was circling and I could see it heading straight toward my friend. Without hesitation, I ran my boat between Jerry and his oncoming boat. With a heavy thud, the runaway boat hit mine and I was able to reach over and turn off his motor.

We became best of friends, and I became his legs for the next three summers. His parents would leave him under my care for the entire summer. He died at the age of twenty-one, but I still fondly remember carrying Jerry on my back up and down the Ozark hills for what I hope he took to his grave as a wonderful memory of his short life. To paraphrase a song: "He wasn't heavy; he was my friend."

<hr>

It was an hour drive to get to Stover from our home. Dad always went to town on Saturdays to get feed for the hogs and groceries. I reckon' I was "perty darn lucky" to get to go with him. After all, I was the oldest son and I felt deserving of a few extra privileges.

I ate my first hamburger at a local bar and grill in downtown Stover when I was thirteen years old. I really thought it had to be the best meal I had ever eaten—it was "manna from heaven." Now, my momma was a decent cook and she made some of the best biscuits ever hand kneaded, but I will never forget my first dill pickled, sliced onions with mustard—hamburger. It was comparable to my first sexual experience, and I swore that when I was grown and had my own money, I was going to eat my fill of hamburgers until I burst!

Grandpa Charlie Capps would go to town with us too, but he would spend most of the day at the tavern and the Ol' Man would spend the rest of his Saturday at the pool hall located several doors down the street. On one particular Saturday, as the story goes, a man came busting into the pool hall and yelled, "Robert! Robert! Willie Metcalf jest hit yer daddy!"

Well the Ol' Man never put up with anyone whoppin' on a kid or an elder, let alone his own dad.

One of life's lessons stressed by my Ol' Man, was "Never start a fight, but never run from one either."

Willie was a known brawler and would scrap at the drop of a hat. Well, by the time the Ol' Man got to the tavern, Willie had run back to his home across town. Dad never lost stride until he walked into the Metcalf home, grabbed Willie by the neck, drug him outside and gave him a lickin' that became legendary, not only in our family, but the entire town of Stover.

⬦

I grew up without a lot of store bought toys. Who needs fancy, store bought toys when you have rocks. Rocks were our first pretend cars and believe me there was "a'plenty" in Ivy Bend.

Most importantly, we had the *woods*. Those magnificent thick groves of cedars, oaks, dogwoods, redbuds, hickories and elms became our playground. Wild grapevines were our swings. I was so proficient on a grapevine that I could ride one across the creek like Tarzan. I never wore a shirt or shoes and I looked the part with my dark tanned skin inherited from my great-great-grandmother Mary Jane Quick. One young cousin believed, in fact, that I *was* Tarzan. The wild grapevines and sumac also provided a canopy for our forts. Best of all was *our* cave. It was the greatest hideout any kid could ask for.

We loved it when our flatland, citified cousins would come from Kansas for a visit. We would scare the bejesus out of them by hiding in the back of "our" cave. One particular cave was our Shangri-La, our spooky, foreboding paradise. All the local hill folk called it Birdsong Cave. It had an opening in the back and the front which afforded us an easy access unbeknownst to those flatlanders—those "prissy, scaredy-cat city slickers." We would lead them through the woods of dead leaning trees and thick over-growth surrounded by natures' noises, strange and mysterious to their ears.

We delighted in preparing them for the scare of their lives; all while my little brother Donnie was sneaking through the backwoods into the back entrance. Once we arrived and made it to the middle of the cave, he began making noises like a wild enraged bear.

It was great entertainment to hear them squealing and crying as they ran out as fast and as far away from the cave as they could. It was a marvel that we didn't actually run onto some real black bears said to inhabit the wilds of the Ozarks during one of our escapades. Like the ones we encountered in Vietnam.

⬦

There are actually two types of bear in Vietnam: Asiatic black bear and Malayan sun bears. Personally, I never saw one, but a soldier I went to boot camp with was out on a patrol and a bear walked up on them. It like to scared them fellers to death.

He told me that later that same night, another soldier wondered off to relieve himself and set off a trip-flare. Trip-flares were road flares connected to wires and activated when the wire was pulled out. These trip flares were set up to secure a perimeter border around a night patrol—to announce any unwanted guests. He came darn close to getting shot by friendly fire!

⬦

Life seemed slower, less complicated and simple back in those childhood days of innocence; maybe the Mennonites yearn to keep life like that for generations to come. Outside influences, sadly, will always pollute their intent and the sway of progress will ultimately lure some of their children away.

It was my good fortune to be raised in the Ivy Bend or as we called it, "Broken Circle." Stealth, in those backwoods became second nature. Sitting quiet amongst the trees was a more religious experience than going to Sunday school and you didn't have to get all gussied up. Shooting a gun was as natural as the flowers bloomin' in springtime. Funny, isn't it, that you just don't appreciate the small pleasures of life until they are memories?

Jimmy and I attended a one-room school in the Ivy-Bend-Proctor area and even had the luxury of a windowless, panel bus that would pick us up and haul us back and forth to school. We always took our guns with us so that on nice days we could walk home and hunt squirrels. Momma appreciated when we brought in some different meat to eat; we all got pretty tired of pork and catfish.

The one room schoolhouse had a wood burning stove right smack dab in the middle of it, so come wintertime we all stayed nice and warm. An enormous fat rat decided to make its home right under the back crawlspace of the building and every now and then, he would make an appearance inside the warm inviting schoolroom lookin' for food. This made a great distraction, and all of us boys would get tickled when the girls would scream and climb up on their seats.

The teacher, Mr. Charles DeJarnette, always had a stack of pinewood paddles and his shotgun propped up in a corner, right next to his desk. One day, he spotted that rat poking his head up from a crack in the floorboards. He motioned us to hush. He rose up from his chair, stealthily grabbed his shotgun and when that rodent dashed across the floor—KAAA-BOOM—the crack of the blast echoed in my ears.

It felt as if the blast of bird shot had passed through both eardrums on its way to the target. I couldn't hear a thing after that explosion, and I know the ringing must have lasted for a week. That big fat rat was splattered all over the back of the wall.

<hr/>

I hated school—too many things to do outside in the sunshine—in the paradise of Ivy Bend. To me, "book learnin' was as useless as tits on a boar hog." Little did I know that my upbringing would eventually save my life.

**Lela Davidson, Charles DeJarnette (teacher), Dad (bus driver); Buzzy Webb, Tommy Capps, Harvey McCollom, Bonnie Luvin, John Henry McCollom (middle); Ray Gene Webb, Ada Purcell, Della Webb, Donna Webb, Raymond Webb, Jimmy Lee Capps, Sonny Webb**
**1955**

# LETTERS HOME

23 Sept 66
1100 hours

Hi Mom, Dad, Kigs.

Well Here I am back at training again. Ive got 6 more days left hear for my final jungl traing then I get to the real thing.

I rote Larry a letter right after I got my address and I should here from hime before to mush longer.

Well anyway we haven't had anything to exciting happen yet and you know I sure as hell glad to.

During the day time around here it gets so darn hot that you can't hardly do a thing then along toward dark it beganes to cool off and then it rains a little while and then it's dark and its realy perty good sleeping for a few hours and I mean a few to. Starting tomorrow were going to be putting in a lot of hours.

I haven't got my mail yet but a cupple of the geyes have the rest of us are paitally weating for our mail to get here.

The whole damn Army over here is made up of gyes from Fort Polk. Any way I sure know a hell of a bunch of these gyes.

The other night Cherly Norris you know from fort Polk any way he went out on a patrol and he said that during the night a bair walk up on them and they all almost died from fright. Then a neither one of the gyes started to take a crap and hit a flair they had sit out as a warning. They were so neverous that they dam near shot that gye. Well its getting perty dark and I gess Im to have to close now and go mail my letters I wrote one to Sally to.

Be sure to tell Mrs. and Mr Wilson Hi for me and I'll try to write the first chance I get. Tell everyone I said Hi.

How is Grapa and Grandamoma? How Gradpa Capps? Has Sonny been drafted yet?

Well I'll right again when I can.

See you in about 51 3/4 weeks just gessing

Tom.

**Tommy, Grandma Whittle, Larry Headley**

## Chapter Four
## The Bishop

Bishop Ezekiel Haldermann appeared to be in his late seventies. He had fathered seventeen children and had earned his esteemed position in his church and community.

Bishop is the title used by several groups of Mennonites in America for the highest ministerial office. The corresponding term in Dutch was *Oudste* (although *bisschop* was also occasionally used) and in German *Aeltester*, English translation "*elder.*" The bishop or elder in the Mennonite Church is the minister who has been ordained to the special charge of caring for and officiating in the church of a certain prescribed district. This district may contain one place of worship, or a number of places, which are at considerable distances from each other.

A bishop may have a number of fellow-ministers in his charge who preach at the various places and aid him in his work generally. Usually the administration of ordination, baptism, marriage, the Lord's Supper, and discipline were exclusive functions of the bishop, along with presiding over the congregation in all its worship and business meetings and pastoral responsibility.

Simply put, Ezekiel Haldermann was the Grand Poohbah over the group of Mennonites that I needed to visit with.

Word had traveled fast and Ezekiel said he was expecting me. As luck would have it, I had actually met Bishop Haldermann before today when I was a milk hauler for a company out of Eldon back in the 1970's. The Haldermann's ran a large dairy at that time, and I picked up their milk and transported it to Jefferson City. It has always been my philosophy to treat everyone, from every walk of life, kind and considerate because you just never know when you might run into that person again and need their kindness and consideration. As my grandpa Capps always said, "Tommy boy, don't ever drop a rusty bucket down a neighbor's well."

Bishop Haldermann was a big man; tall in stature, with an initial unyielding appearance, but once he warmed up to you, he was a soft-spoken gentle giant. His tawny wrinkled face was well worn from years of hard work in the sun, wind, rain and snow. His eyes were barely visible through the folds of his droopy eyelids, yet there was a kindness emanating from his pale blue eyes.

He led me onto his front porch and gestured that I should take a seat. The day had gotten hotter than predicted, so the cool breeze and shade was a welcome respite. The Bishop's wife came to the door offering us fresh squeezed lemonade. I have to admit, the tart, yet sweet, liquid tasted like nectar from heaven. I don't believe I have ever tasted such delicious lemonade.

Several of his grandchildren came running around the corner of the house, and without speaking a word, he swooshed them away with a stern look and a wave of his hand. His knuckles were gnarled and twisted from arthritis and a lifetime of manual labor. Those hands told the story of one pious man.

My thoughts wandered to another gentle giant who quickly came into my life and was gone with the instantaneous pull of a trigger. A replacement had joined us in Company B. He was a giant of a man too! He towered over all of us at six foot ten inches, and we nicknamed our black brother "Big Bad John" after the song made famous by Jimmy Dean. We never bothered too much with learning proper first or last names; not many lived long enough nor escaped serious injuries while serving in Company B.

No one wanted to get too attached.

I have heard statistics that in WWII an infantryman averaged ten days of combat per year; in Vietnam, an infantryman averaged 240 combat days per year. This proved all too true for Big Bad John. His hands were so enormous they dwarfed the M-60 machine gun that he carried like an M-16 rifle. His stature ultimately cost him his life.

We were out on one of our search and destroy patrols when we ran into random gunfire from the bush—we all hit the ground. We had been moving in our typical T formation with Big Bad John in the middle of the main column of the T. Two men humped security to the right of him while I was humping left security. The enemy bullets ripped through the jungle's bamboo overgrowth and found their marks. Providence once again had smiled down on me, sparing me for another day, another battle.

But, Big Bad John was an easy target, and the bullets met up with the top of his head. It was an awful sight; one of those sights that once imprinted in your brain can never be erased. His skull hung half-blown off and brain matter splattered in random patterns on the jungle floor where he took his last breath.

Two other nameless combat infantry brothers rested peacefully on the Vietnam jungle floor. Death came so instantaneously that they appeared to have merely laid down on the ground for an afternoon nap.

The ironic thing about this attack was that we never saw one combatant! Another statistic, not lost on this soldier, was that 153,329 Americans were hospitalized for wounds suffered in Vietnam, and 99% of those who made it through the first twenty-four hours survived.

We dutifully made litters out of our half-shelters, with four of us hooked onto corners to carry out their bodies. Being pretty far into the jungle on that fateful day, we had a long dangerous challenge ahead of us. Humping uphill, we would slide back down on the leaking blood. Our canvas boots would absorb the blood and stick in the mud of the jungle floor. The litters were soaked and dripping blood. Our entire bodies were drenched with sweat and blood, and our eyes were constantly scanning our surroundings hoping to spot the enemy before they spotted us.

We humped about five klicks until we eventually hooked up with our company. Nightfall was upon us as we entered the camp. We must have presented a horrifying sight in the fading light. They all assumed that everyone had been wounded because of our baptism in blood and human matter.

Exhaustion hit and I collapsed as we respectfully lowered the body of "Big Bad John" to the ground. I dropped to the ground, unable to move, with my head resting on his body. The lyrics of an old hillbilly song, "Oh, Death, Oh Death, Won't You Spare Me," that my uncles Sid Luvin, Wilford Whittle and Melvon Whittle mournfully sang many a night around a coon hunt campfire echoed in my ears, its meaning more clear. No one escapes death; the hand of death will open the final door for each of us to either heaven or hell.

We secured an area for a helicopter to land that next day to retrieve their bodies for their long trip home. I never grieved outwardly over there; I figured grieving was a sign of weakness. I grieved inwardly for a country losing their youth and for the families that made the ultimate sacrifice. I guess the Good Book states "Greater love hath no man than this, that a man lay down his life for his friends"—but I would add for what purpose? And to what purpose did God allow me to live?

By the end of my first month, almost half of the men I started with had been wounded or killed in action. Death was almost an everyday occurrence when you were an infantryman; simply put, it was their unlucky day. Or was it "their time"?

I have never believed in predestination and in this situation, I was just fortunate to be walking ten feet to the left of them. I never wanted to die; I wanted to do my duty and go back home. But, sometimes my thoughts begged the question, "Why was I spared to fight another day?"

<hr />

I let the bishop make the first comment about the "Dutch Country Rapes," as they came to be called. We had discussed crops, cattle and hogs and I knew, out of respect, I should let him bring up the subject.

Ezekiel began, "Are you familiar with the Book of Ephesians, Tommy? In particular, Chapter 5, Verse 12 says, '*It is a shame even to speak of those things which are done of them in secret.'* But today...today, men seem to delight in exploiting the innocent by succumbing to the devil's bidding. You know, Tommy, we have all types of people, just like you English. We are not perfect, no one is." He continued, "This is an inconceivable act upon our innocent children and I want it stopped."

The bishop paused for several seconds, and then he said, "Tommy, you find who is responsible for these crimes, whether it is one of our fold or not, and you have *permission* to do what needs to be done." With a loud voice he interjected, "But! Only you will question our children."

There you have it; once again, without uttering a single word about the incidents, I had succeeded in gaining the confidence of this Mennonite leader to proceed with my investigation.

**Melvon, Vinson and Wilford Whittle, 1983**

**Melvon and Wilford Whittle, 1947**

# LETTERS HOME

25 Sept 66<br>2030 hours

Hi Everybody

Well are you all doing your shar of holding down Missouri for me. I sure hope so because man Im coming back there before you gyes ever mise me. Hows Everbody making it? They have got some of our mail screw up some where along the line and well im sure you people know how the Army does things any way. Hows Dad feeling? Is Gradma and grampa still at your house? Say Hi to them for me and tell them I would write but Im so darn bussy that bye the time I write to my wife I don't have mush time left. Hows Grapa Capps? Hows Mr. and Mrs. Wilson?

Did Sonny get Drafted yet? Did he get another car?

I would write to him but I almost know that he'll be in the Army before he would get my letter. Tell him if he's still at home Hi for me.

Its been raining almost evey night and around some of these tents mud is about knee deep in most places.

We have had two gyes shoot them selves in the foot just to get out of here and both of them shot them selves today. We had another gye jump out of a helacopter and knock a big hole in his knee. And another to grab a hot M-16 barrol and burn his hand and two others stept on booby traps which just took all the hide of off one boys foot and lower leg and the other gye got about half of his tooes took off. I think we must have set some kind of record because were just suspose to be in a jungle school and in 5 days out of 87 men we have had 6 gyes get hurt bad enough to go to the hospital and not come back.

Hows the kigs like school? I have got a lot of frends who I knew from fort Polk and two who I knew from fort Leonord Wood. When my time goes to getting short I may get extended 30 days and then E.T.S. when I get back to the states. Although that's a long time off to come.

Has the weather got or getting cooler yet? Man here it gets up to about 95 or 100 everyday and the humidity is about 0 or 95 and man that makes it realy hot. And inless were in a rubber plantation we never have any shade of any kind neither. And when it rains boy it rains over here.

Tell Mr. and Mrs. Wilson that I'll try to write them the first chance I get but from the looks of things it will be at lest 3 days before I can and pobley longer. Well I better close and go to bed because there won't be any sleeping tomorrow night.

Goodnight.
Your all's Son
The Solger.

Tom

Did Jimmy get a car yet?

Has Pete and Roy got there House Started up yet?
Tell them I said Hi. And tell Roy I haven't been a hero
for him yet. Im still a chicken—Like Hell—But I do
get scard

**Linda, Terri, Donnie, Jimmy,
Tommy, Mitchell, Marshall**

# Chapter Five
## Lost Innocence

The Zuckholders were expecting me, and as I pulled my car into their lane, their dogs ran out to greet me—excitedly barking and jumping on my clean pair of pants. I made a quick mental note that I must remember to ask them about their dogs and if all strangers were greeted likewise. I had phoned ahead wanting to make sure that I got their statements while it remained fresh in their memories and to give them a chance to prepare for my intrusion into their lives. I also needed to record a complete walk through of the events of that October night with Kristin and her parents.

I decided that first of all it would be best to have everyone else out of the home except Kristin and Eva Ruth, but as plans go, Jacob insisted that he be the *only* one with his daughter. So Eva Ruth sat out on the porch snapping green beans, watching her other children run carefree and barefoot in the last warm rays of the fall sunshine.

I asked Kristin to show me her bedroom. No one had slept there since the deed, as the Dutchies referred to it, and the beds remained unmade. The open windows allowed a rush of fresh breeze that billowed the sheer curtains outward as if trying to absorb and expel all of the evil from the room. Kristin had such a panicked, hurt look on her face, and she nervously sucked on the end of one of her long braids of hair.

I knelt down and reassured her that I would do my best to make sure that the bad man would never hurt her again. She looked like a little angel in her ankle length, cotton flowered dress. I explained as simply as possible to her that I intended to find the man who had hurt her, but it would require using a video camera and require her to tell her story exactly as it happened. I also explained that the video could be viewed by others and ultimately used as a tool to bring peace of mind and safety to her community.

Interviewing a child requires a patient demeanor and an empathetic heart. A child's vocabulary contains hundreds of words compared to an adult's thousands. I always initiate my conversations with questions about their favorite color or food or pets. By doing this, I am able to discern their level of comprehension and their ability to answer plausibly.

Understanding a child's body language is also key to a successful interview. Perception and the ability to channel my total attention to a child are essential in gaining their trust. I have seen college educated experts with all kinds of letters at the end of their names fail at attempts to interrogate children because they don't understand the concept of "simple."

I began my questioning in an unrushed, soft-spoken manner, "Kristin, will you please tell me everything that you remember on the evening of October 20th?"

"I was dreaming when he woke me," she began. "I felt his hand brush across my face. He had a strange smell." Kristin's voice faltered, but she continued, "Then he said, 'God has sent me to give you a baby.' He lifted me up out of my bed and carried me downstairs. He said, 'Don't be afraid, I won't hurt you, God sent me. Don't be scared.'"

This was the first that I had heard that the alleged rape didn't take place in her bedroom. Kristin, in a low whisper said, "But this time he did hurt me. He pulled off my panties. I tried to call out for my mommy when he got on top of me. I couldn't breathe!"

Without hesitation, the story poured out of her tiny soul. "He covered my mouth with his hand and said if I made any noise that God would have him kill my mom and dad and my sisters."

Kristin looked sad and bewildered and I hated this monster. I actually hate all the deviant monsters that prey on children, but this one...this *one,* I especially hated.

"It wasn't like all the other nights he visited me. He usually just felt my hair and ran his hands up and down my legs. This time..." she paused, "This time he tried to stick me with his pickle."

Parents use lots of names for "the male private areas." I have heard it called a tally-whacker, a peter, a willy, but never a pickle.

Jolted by Kristin's statement and the newly acquired knowledge that he had been there multiple times, Jacob and I stood silently in shock. Never leading in an interview with a child, I encouraged her to continue.

Staring downward, Kristin said, "He tried and tried to poke me and I was crying. He quit and I opened my eyes to see him grab his pickle and he began rubbing it. He was saying, *'Prijzen God almachtig, Halleluiah, Halleluiah.'*"

"Wait a second, did he talk Dutch?" I asked.

Kristin nodded her head yes. Without encouragement, Kristin continued, "He fell on top of me and something warm ran onto my tummy. He said, 'Next time I will give you a baby.' Then after a while, he picked me up and carried me back to my bed."

It is difficult, if not impossible, to think that another Mennonite could be the perpetrator, and I never jump to conclusions until all the evidence is presented. I would be back another day, and Kristin was exhausted after giving such a detailed statement for her young age.

Driving back to the office in Jefferson City a soft rain began tapping on my windshield; I became lost in another decade—another lost innocence.

⎯⎯◇⎯⎯

God, it was raining again, darkness had settled on the jungle. Me and eleven others were out on yet another ambush patrol. I was chosen as a triggerman on this particular night. It was a moonless night, but come to think of it, I don't remember one night of moonlight while I was in Country. I do remember being so tired whenever we were lucky enough to be in a base camp that I would fall asleep standing straight up. *But*, not tonight—tonight as ambush triggerman, my brothers were counting on me to be alert.

I carefully chose a position that would afford me a clear field-of-fire at a crossroad of bush trails. All twelve of us lay prostrate on the jungle floor—ants, centipedes, bugs and leeches ever present. The incessant night sounds of the jungle seemed to penetrate our brains, trying their best to drive us to madness. The bush crickets were unremitting; the penetrating expletive of the "fuck-you" lizards chimed in with its namesake call, and the shrill night cries of the monkeys joined the chorus. If you let it, the noise was deafening—*we had to hear beyond the clutter*, our lives depended upon it.

Our weapons made ready. The rain had stopped and our ponchos were secured tightly to make the least amount of noise when we needed to readjust our bodies. My eyes adjusted to the blackness and I settled in. In the black of the landscape, we relied on "sound" as the enemy soldiers would attempt intentionally, or accidentally, to enter the American night defensive positions.

This was my typical ambush patrol that occurred every three days. I had been in this position for nearly three long, unnerving hours when I heard slow and deliberate footsteps in the underbrush across the road. Two Vietnamese insurgents passed the intersection. Being aware of the Viet Cong patrol maneuvers, I held my fire, and my breath, believing them to be the point element of a much larger guerrilla force. I could hear my own heart beat in my eardrums, and my breathing sounded as if I was exhaling a hurricane.

I waited what seemed like an eternity until the enemy platoon of twenty men eased up the jungle path lined with my buddies. My body, excruciatingly constrained, was tense and anxious. Releasing all my pent up nerves and stored adrenaline, I directed an intense barrage of fire upon the bulk of them, killing many of the young Viet Cong soldiers.

Everyone else came alive with my initiation and united in the exchange of bullets. The rest of the enemy soldiers scattered into the blackness of the dense bush. In the chaos of the moment, I ran out to retrieve what I could from the bodies. This had to be done immediately, because we had to leave as quickly as possible. It was crucial after a firefight to get the hell out of the area or you risked becoming the ambushed.

I dodged several bullets and returned the favor in the direction of the sniper fire, and a brief dead silence shrouded the jungle. I was able to secure several documents and weapons—this earned me an Army Commendation Medal with "V" Device.

"Valor, Bravery?" Heck, I was just doing my job, but I was proud that I could do my duty as the triggerman.

My explanation, to anyone who asks, is that *my* individual war was fought in a twelve foot square. I became so focused on what was happening directly in my space that all other action seemed as suspended animation on each side of my narrow field of vision, as if I was wearing clear horse blinders. I was just a nineteen-year-old E-1 or 2, and I never knew where I was or where I was being sent. Only afterward—after the shooting stopped, the dead were counted and left behind and a pseudo-golden dawn broke—did the entire picture of my war become vivid.

"It was never my intention to be valorous." Omar Bradley, U. S. Army General during World War II said it best, *"Bravery is the capacity to perform properly even when scared half to death."*

DEPARTMENT OF THE ARMY

THIS IS TO CERTIFY THAT
THE SECRETARY OF THE ARMY HAS AWARDED

THE ARMY COMMENDATION MEDAL

WITH "V" DEVICE

TO

PRIVATE FIRST CLASS TOMMY R. CAPPS, US55841739, UNITED STATES ARMY

FOR

HEROISM IN THE REPUBLIC OF VIETNAM ON 21 NOVEMBER 1966

GIVEN UNDER MY HAND IN THE CITY OF WASHINGTON
THIS TWENTY-SIXTH DAY OF JANUARY 19 67

W. E. DePUY
Major General, USA
Commanding

Stanley R. Resor
SECRETARY OF THE ARMY

# LETTERS HOME

6 or 7 Oct 66
1600 hours

Hi Mom & kigs & DAD

Well I haven't got to mush time Ive got to get my
dirty loandary together and send it off today yet.

We have been out on the field for 5 or 6 days and
Ive just got in last night leaving again in the morning.
So as you probly know it will probley be a few more
days before you here from me again so don't get
excited if you don't get a letter for a few days. Hows
everbody? Be sure to tell grandma that I'll write to
her the first chance I get but Im so push for time now
I just haven't got time.

My job in our squad is Assisant machine gunner
when were in a posistation and right sercerty when
we are moving. Im proud to be in the big red one but
you can tell dad Im not trying to be any hero or
anything but I haven't been scared yet and we have
had few incidints but nothing big or bad.

Although I am a little more nervous than I used to
be. And everytime I here a pop I bite the dust and I
bet Dad knows what Im talking about to.

Well everbody I gess this is perty short but I have
to get my loundry done or I will realy be a strong arm
boy around here stinking that is Ive got on my last
clean set of cloths now.

Your all's Ken
Tom
PS Tell grapa Capps Hi
   Hows Dad?
I know this letter is dirty but forget the dirt on it, its perty muddy around here in some places.

## Chapter Six
## Don't Look Back

The word was spreading like wild fire in the Mennonite community. The phone lines lit up at the office as parents began calling with the same sad stories about their daughters' sexual encounters with a man in their own homes. All in all, six new victims came forward. The perpetrator always used the same phrases and threats—"God has sent me to give you a baby," and "If you tell anyone I will kill your family."

In my career, I have dealt with many horrible men and women whose demented souls were so twisted with perversion that they were beyond God's repentance. They were preachers, teachers, babysitters and even cops, but never had I ever heard of using God to coerce and violate young innocent girls. Would they ever trust again? Would their outlook on life always be haunted with undesirable memories?

I had to suppress my inner demons to keep from jumping across the interview tables and strangling each of the perverts that I interrogated. I always treated them with my "good ol' boy" persona and always at the conclusion of a videotaped interview, I would reach over and shake their hands. This always blocked a defense attorney from claiming I used undue coercion or intimidation to obtain the perpetrator's statement.

<hr/>

I was told that the Dutch have a fable of the spider and his web, and it goes something like this: There was once a young spider who peered down from the dark peak of a barn to a beam below that was showered with sunlight. The spider began to spin a long strong fiber that would allow him to settle on the beam. He was so happy with his new accommodations that he decided to build his home, and the spider created a beautiful, strong web where he caught many flies and lived in the comfort of his home.

Many years passed, and he wondered why there was a long strand of web leading up into the darkness. Believing he no longer needed the strand, he bit it in two. His home collapsed. Is this analogy the paradox of our faith? I like to believe that the thin strand of promise in our faith becomes our anchor line of hope for the future.

<hr/>

Psalm Hooper was his next and, ultimately, his last victim. This child rapist knew that his crimes were being investigated, but like most pedophiles, he relished the prospect of public knowledge.

I worked for months in St. Louis on a worldwide child porn network called *The Cheshire Cat* during my rookie days with STAT. I learned early on that most pedophiles delight in taking souvenirs from their victims and leaving minute traces of evidence to divert investigators in the wrong direction. You don't need a degree in psychology to know that they crave attention and notoriety for their perverse deeds.

Psalm was twelve, but a bit shy and backward. I don't mean that in a negative way, just slow to answer questions and as jittery as a scared barn kitten. I have come a long way from the backwoods of Ivy Bend to the Vietnam private to the state investigator. I never received a college education, but with years of work experience and hours upon hours of training, I earned the reputation of an investigator who got his perpetrator with common sense and empathy.

***

I was often called "backward" or "stupid" in a negative way by my younger brother Jimmy, but that is how most brothers communicate their love. I always accused him of being nothing short of a "smartass." I am proud now to say that he was the first in my family to get a college degree.

I was just sixteen when I decided to quit school. I felt awkward and lost sitting in a classroom and besides, I was flunking every subject. My reading was so poor that I could not comprehend the meaning of a sentence, let alone a paragraph. At the age of sixteen, I cast aside *"learnin' for shovelin'."*

My first backbreaking occupation was digging water line ditches with a pick and shovel in the hard, rocky, godforsaken ground of Ivy Bend. I was working for my uncle Sid Luvin and earning seventy-five cents an hour. In hindsight, it was the best workout program ever created, and I became one muscle bound young man.

My next job was working for a lawn service in Kansas City with my best friend Sonny Webb. I brought in a whopping salary of seventy-five dollars per week, and I guarantee you it was more than a forty-hour week. Sonny was more fit and muscle bound than I ever hoped to be.

Once, when we were trimming a tree, a forked branch fell over a telephone wire and hung like a wishbone balanced on a string. The boss barked out an order, "Sonny, take a ladder and lean it up against the wire and lift that branch off."

Well, you can just imagine what happened after he lifted the branch's weight off that wire. Yes sir, it flung straight up taunt, like a scene in a Laurel and Hardy movie, leaving Sonny clutching the ladder now suspended in midair, glaring eye to eye with me and the boss.

We all learned a fast lesson in the laws of gravity that day as he rode that ladder clear down to the ground. Sonny and the ladder hit the ground with a jarring thud.

Looking down at Sonny the boss yelled, "Sonny, Sonny, are you all right?"

Sonny, with fire in his eyes, yelled back, "Hell yes, I'm all right."

The boss stifled a chuckle, and I warned him, "Don't you dare laugh; Sonny will climb straight up this tree and whip your ass or cut down this tree with us in it!"

<hr/>

I married my first wife on February 21, 1966, the same day I received my draft notice. The draft found me and everyone else not smart enough to stay in school in 1966. I gave my bride-to-be the option of not marrying me, since I didn't know when, or even *if,* I would return. In retrospect, I wonder if my young age and my experiences in Vietnam doomed both of my previous marriages.

I was inducted into the U.S. Army on March 21, 1966. It was when I was over in Vietnam that I made a solemn promise to myself, "If I live through this, by God, I am going back to school, graduate and get my diploma."

<hr/>

My job now was not to rush through this investigation, but I also did not want the trail to grow cold. It was a gloomy, cloudy and dark Monday morning when I met with Psalm at her grandparent's home. Psalm had not had the courage to return to her home, and her parents were patiently supporting her decision to remain with her grandparents.

She sat in a wooden rocking chair, wringing her little hands and hurriedly rocking back and forth while I sat up the video camera. She was not very eager to tell her story, and I had the feeling that it was going to be a struggle to pull detailed information from her.

Psalm was adopted from the Foster/Adopt program ran by the state of Missouri. I have been told that because of marrying relatives, many Mennonite couples are sterile or their infant children die of a so-called *"maple syrup"* disease; so named because the urine of a baby born to a closely related couple smells sweet like maple syrup.

So now many of the families choose to adopt to acquire new blood lines for their society. They are great parents and raise up children the way the English did in the 1950's—with respect for people and their property. My wife Teresa licensed Foster/Adopt families in her career with Children's Division, and she always bragged on how the Mennonite families could succeed with a difficult or *"behavioral"* child who had not succeeded in English foster homes.

Teresa reiterated often that Mennonites possess a gentle strictness with the authoritative control to merely articulate a soft reprimand to a child who will comply immediately with obedience. But they also adhered to the Bible teaching of "Spare the rod and spoil the child." The state, however, had strict guidelines that prohibited any physical punishment of foster children. Teresa taught Foster/Adopt classes and recommended the reading of *The Horse Whisperer*.

The Mennonites also have a prison baby program called Tender Touches from which they can eventually adopt the babies born to women serving prison sentences. The Tender Touches program is only available for Mennonite families, and more often than not, when incarcerated mothers are released from prison they never return for their children.

If they do return, no matter how long the child has been raised in a Mennonite home, the mother has the legal right to her child. This has caused many a broken heart. But, that explains why you will now see a diverse Mennonite community.

Upon my cue, Psalm began to tell her story, "I can't remember if I have ever seen him before he visited, but he came into my room on Saturday night. Sunday is my favorite day; we go to church and then usually to my grandma's for dinner. Then back to church for singing."

Her story began somewhat chaotic and jumbled, like a bee flitting from one flower to the next, but I knew better than to interrupt when she was opening up. "I love to sing and my name is from the book of Psalm in the Bible!" she exclaimed.

In the Mennonite churches, the women and young children sit on the left side segregated from the men folk on the right side. Gender roles in the Mennonite community are clearly defined—women cook, clean, care for babies, tend garden, mow the grass and make most all of the clothing. Women are to be subservient—unlike the majority of English society, but they are treated with respect, love and admiration. I was told that if there is the slightest evidence of domestic abuse, the church elders intervene. Rest assured, as in all societies, Mennonite women are the backbone of the family and subtly maintain order.

Keeping Miss Psalm on track might prove to be a challenge, so I redirected her to tell me about the events of Saturday night.

Psalm thought a moment and began again, "I thought I heard a noise, but I thought maybe someone forgot to take something on the campout. My family was going camping at the creek just down the road, and I did not want to go." Pausing briefly she loudly exclaimed, "I will go next time!" Breathlessly, Psalm blurted out, "I won't ever stay by myself again!"

She told me, almost verbatim, what each and every other little victim had told me. "He told me God sent him to me to give me a baby." Psalm continued, "He told me to never, never say one word about his visit, because he had been sent by God to put a baby in my tummy. He whispered in my ear, 'If you ever say a word to anyone, God will make me kill your family.'"

Tears ran down her freckled cheeks and dripped onto her pink cotton dress. Her head drooped, and the untied flowered bonnet slid forward, hiding her pale bluish-green eyes. "I was so scared," she said resolutely.

Being a very obedient and frightened child, Psalm lay awake the rest of the night awaiting the first golden rays of morning sunlight.

Fretfully, she explained how she quietly crawled out of her bed at daylight and made her way over to her bedroom window, which was directly over the porch roof. Scared that he was still in the house, she quickly opened the window and lowered herself to the roof wearing only her nightgown and panties. Psalm jumped to the ground and ran across the field to her grandparent's home.

Psalm added emphatically, "I never looked back! I ran through the cornfield as fast as I could, and it was so muddy that I felt as if I would sink and get stuck." Psalm had braved the quarter mile sprint barefooted to collapse into the sanctuary of her grandfather's loving arms.

⊷⬥⬦⬥⊶

Vivid recollections of sprinting five klicks through the Vietnam jungle with a forty-pound ruck flooded my thoughts. There comes a time in life and war when the only option to save yourself is to run...and run you must, as fast as your legs can carry you!

It was another day of "search and destroy" patrolling in the bush—only difference—it was a bright, sunny day. Our squad of fifteen men was humping in our typical double cross pattern when the RTO (radio telephone operator) suddenly gave us the command to immediately retreat. He had just been informed that we were walking head on toward a fast advancing company of three hundred Viet Cong soldiers.

The Viet Cong had adopted guerrilla warfare tactics and had no real base, unless it was underground. I was always an obedient soldier until the day we blundered onto the opening of one of their underground tunnels. My sergeant ordered me to go down the hole. I flat out refused and contemptuously challenged his authority. "Fuck you! I ain't goin' down there," was my only reply. I was adamant, and he was going to have to kill me before I crawled into that viper pit.

That was the one and only time I ever refused a command. Luckily for me, another soldier quickly volunteered. Honestly, I was not a glory seeker, and I sure as hell didn't want to die in a hole in Vietnam.

You didn't have to tell this country boy twice to retreat; no one looked back as I and the rest of the squad turned tail and ran. With all our might we sprinted, M-16's clutched to our chests, boots barely touching the earth, escaping the certain death that once approached us, back through the thick undergrowth toward a cleared helicopter landing zone.

The landing zone was now between us and a U.S. Artillery Base. Coordinates were being called in while we were fleeing, and 155 mm Howitzers instantly began deploying their volleys of death precisely behind us. Tactics of the guerilla Viet Cong were referred to as "hanging onto the belts of the Americans," that is to say, they tried to stay close so that when we used air support we would kill our own men.

If you can imagine the loudest clap of directly overhead thunder you have ever heard, well my friend, that is the sound of a 155 mm Howitzer explosion. We all knew damn well there was airborne shrapnel cutting through the jungle just beyond our heels. You could hear a rattle and a whooshing wind noise from the giant Howitzer projectiles heading through the tops of the trees and hammering the earth with a deafening detonation. Then, just two-thirds of the way to the landing zone the sniper fire began buzzing past our heads.

Helicopters had already landed at the zone and wasted no time in evacuating us back to our company. Fear is motivation; Fear is the beast that feeds on attention, and in my opinion, Fear is also an innate strength.

**Sonny Webb and Tommy Capps**

# LETTERS HOME

Oct 16 - 66

17:00

Hi Eveyone

Well we are finaly back at home base so I gess I might be able to catch upon a few letter's and maby tell you people a few things. First of all our home base is here at Phouc Vinh that is about 40 miles Nortwest of Seigon so you should know just about where I am.

I got a letter from Linda today. I was real glad to here from her. Has Sally came home yet she didn't say anything about it in my letter but I know her purty good so I figured that there a 50% chance that she would probly be there before to long.

We are suspose to get a few days off for about a week then we are going down south for a few days so I may get a chance to rest a little although we are on bergade stand bye and if anything happens we are the first ones to be called in to help.

In Sonnys letter he describe his car and man it realy sounded tough. I think I'd really like to have that thing just to speed around in.

How's your car holding up? Hows your money holding? I gess its probley getting perty cool over there now. Man its getting other is anything over here. It used to rain evey day and night here now it only rains about avey other night but that's a plenty when your laying out in the jungle or a poncho under the stars but realy after a week you get used to it. I can just lay down anywhere and sleep but I do sleep awful light most of the time.

Well its about time for chow so I gess I'll close for now and mabey I can write more later on but if I can't you all take it easy and I'll sure see you gyes in about a—well us not put it that way I'll see you before long

Love To you all
Tom
The Solger boy

P S.

By the way Ive got me a nick name of Andy almost everyone call me Andy.

PS

I got out of that dern weapon squad now I am a rifle man. Not any more safe but at lest they don't try to kill me by carring amo and cleaning machine gun all time and digging a better position for the damn thing.

You all take care see you all
Tom

# Chapter Seven
## Irony?

As heartbreaking as this job can be, I was determined to get more information from Psalm today. We continued on, slowly and meticulously with the interview.

The assault took place on a moonlit night and Psalm saw what the man looked like. She described him as having blond hair, pale blue eyes and small in stature, not much bigger than herself. As the others also described he was dirty and the smell of sweat, oil or gasoline was prominent.

Psalm ended her tragic story with a new and sickening detail—he had forced her to perform oral sex. I don't know why this case was so repulsive to me—I guess because these innocent, God-fearing children did not deserve to be violated so reprehensibly.

All abusive acts against children are reprehensible. It is truly heart wrenching, the extreme depths of cruelty a power-seeking human being can inflict upon the weak and the innocent. It can break the human spirit when everything they believe and all that they value is lost. Trust is a resilient virtue; nonetheless, it takes time and forgiveness to regain once trust is desecrated.

I have worked cases that are the crux of nightmares. I have read articles asserting that a psychopath's brain is wired differently; that the diagnosable psychopath has no empathy, no remorse and no impulse control. Could evil then be inherent? Must evil exist in order for the mentally and emotionally healthy human being to show compassion? If one believes we live in a world under divine control, I question why evil should exist at all.

The Mennonite religion and all Christian religions teach complete forgiveness of evil doers; perhaps, I like to believe, we need to know evil to overcome evil.

The vilest case I can remember was a cannibalistic preacher who lured in transsexual boys with the advertisement and promise of free surgery. The surgery consisted of being drugged, tied up and removal of their unwanted genitals with hedge clippers—all videotaped. Sad and depraved; sadder still, no one ever came forward to identify the bodies of these young boys. Another example is the case where parents used their four children in home "kiddie porn" movies with a midget porn star who went by the pseudonym, Tripod.

The depravity of some humans is beyond all comprehension and the "church-goer" with blinders will find it very hard indeed to believe that such evil exists in this world. But it does. And it happens in small rural communities as well as in big cities.

The last thirteen years of my law enforcement career was spent with STAT. I would kiss the devil on the lips, and many times, I did to bring justice for the victims. Fuck forgiveness! I find the ultimate satisfaction and contentment in knowing that these perpetrators will spend the rest of their lives behind bars and "will do no evil" to their victims ever again.

Psalm repeated his last command before he disappeared from her room, "Do not move until the sun comes up or God will order me to kill all of your family." And as the others had described Psalm reiterated, "He spoke using some Dutch words." Life is full of ironic situations and I have experienced more than my share.

— ❈ —

The first base camp I was stationed at had a Vietnamese barber. He was a jovial little man, always smiling and nodding affirmatively to the soldiers lined up daily to get their haircuts and shaves. There were all types of Vietnamese workers at the U.S. base camps; however, they all had to leave camp before sunset.

It was common practice for the Viet Cong to try to sneak up on the base camp at night and turn the claymores around to face their blast toward the American camps when detonated. M18 claymore anti-personnel mines were created to maim or kill enemy ground troops approaching a position from a specific direction and were primarily used by us infantrymen in protecting the perimeter guards. We also used claymores on ambush patrols, strategically placing them along well-known Viet Cong paths.

These claymores were a beneficial tool when we found ourselves in close quarters with the enemy and didn't want them to sneak up on our position.

Claymores were connected to our foxholes or trenches with a wire joined to a plunger similar to a dynamite plunger. The other end was connected to a fuse inserted into C-4, a rope explosive that could be molded like putty and placed inside the claymore. The advantage of such a weapon was in the widespread dispersal of lethal steel ball bearings up to a distance of a hundred yards.

One night there was a commotion out by the perimeter with several shots fired and claymores detonated. Often the enemy would attempt to stealthily clip the wires of the claymores and steal them or, as I explained previously, turn them around to kill Americans when detonated.

The next morning the bodies of three Vietnamese were found, including one body missing his legs who had pulled himself to the edge of the jungle leaving a blood trail. This was the base barber. Like I've said before, I could not feel remorse for an enemy combatant and certainly not toward a person that had held a straight razor to my neck a few days before.

But I often question how a person that had at least acted like a comrade could do such a thing? I've asked myself that question hundreds of times in my law enforcement career and to this day, I haven't found the answer. Perhaps the solution is simply to be the best person you can be to those around you, even when that person may be "sneaking in" to hurt you. Perhaps kind-heartedness will turn their hearts to the right.

Life as an infantryman was sometimes mundane and boring. On the other hand, sometimes soldiering became a life or death matter—the extreme contrasts are the fundamentals of a combat soldier's psyche.

Another listening post night was assigned with the lieutenant and sergeants directing us to our position sites. This particular base camp was set smack dab in the middle of a rubber plantation. We had found an old foxhole—two foot deep, four foot wide and eight foot long. It was just after dusk, when within the surrounding rubber trees, I saw three figures stealthily take cover behind the trees and a termite hill. Termite hills in Vietnam were massive, rock hard and they made excellent cover and protection from bullets.

The three men were in the "kill zone." Quickly I keyed the radio with two quick clicks of the button. This was the signal designated to alert the camp. No one answered. I tried again—to no avail—and the figures approached closer, heading toward us and the base camp.

With hand signals, I relayed the urgency for action to the two soldiers beside me. I cut loose on the three figures assuming they were the point of an entire company. The base camp came to life as did the enemy soldiers coming toward us. We were caught in the crossfire. Bark from the rubber trees flew into our foxhole as we cautiously returned fire, briefly exposing our heads and position.

With each weapon exchange, they precisely located our position and pitched a hand grenade meticulously right to the edge of our foxhole. We all bent over in a fetal position, covering our heads, waiting for the explosion. Miraculously, it didn't explode!

I thought to myself, by God, I can throw a hand grenade too! Quickly rising up, I pulled the pin out of the grenade and counted to two before I hurled it forward with the skill of a baseball player hitting the sweet spot of the strike zone. It exploded, meeting its mark—the shooting stopped.

Out of the dark quiet came the shouts of cuss words and yells of U.S. Army soldiers. They shouted out information about their division and that they were an Army unit that had gotten off course of their coordinates. They were on their way to an ambush patrol.

Inadvertently, or incompetently, they had walked directly into our kill zone. Luckily for those men, there was a termite hill and a berm of hard jungle soil between them and all the bullets.

Thank God, only three of our men were wounded that night by friendly fire. I don't know why, but once again, my guardian angel had saved my life. Life and death—that thin line separated by a compass needle reading and a dud hand grenade. The company commander chewed our asses, asserting his disgust with their ineptness, "You should have killed the entire bunch of stupid sons-of-bitches."

<hr/>

Psalm's grandmother entered the room, drying her hands on her apron commonly worn over the Dutchy dresses, bringing my attention back to the business at hand.

Her grandmother's gray hair was tucked neatly in a bun under a prayer "kapp" or what we English refer to as "coffee filters." I am told that Mennonite women wear these prayer caps in obedience to the commands given in 1st Corinthians. These commands are that a Christian woman should have long uncut hair and that it should be modestly covered with a veil signifying her submissiveness under the authority of her husband or father.

Her dark colored dress and black stockings contrasted sharply to Psalm's pastel attire. She greeted me with a half-smile and a questioning look, to which I nodded in the affirmative. She went to Psalm and picking her up, held her in a tight, loving embrace. Adopted or not, unconditional love is a pillar of the Mennonite faith.

Psalm began to cry and shake uncontrollably. Between sobs, she pitifully asked the question, "Will I have a baby now?"

"Only God knows," her grandmother answered in a hushed, soothing voice. Again she repeated, "Only God knows and we do not question his will."

Before leaving their home, the grandparents provided me with a brown paper sack containing Psalm's gown and underpants. It was 1998 and with the prominence of the 1994 O. J. Simpson trial, DNA evidence was becoming a valuable proof of innocence or guilt in criminal cases. I had tried to educate all involved in the Dutch community as to the importance of saving obvious evidence and not contaminating physical evidence. Psalm's parents had also saved the bed sheets and blankets.

Driving away, I contacted the office to once again send out the state helicopter to look for footprints or any other evidence they could spot in the muddy fields between the two homes.

# LETTERS HOME

17 Oct 66

19:25 hours

Hi Everone,

Well here I am sitting in a nice dry tent with electric lighting and I a wood floor. It rained today and bye goly it sure nice to be here to espacily scence its raing.

Im realy glad to here about Sonny and I hope the hell he never has to go. Tell him he's better write me or I'll kick his ass good when I get back.

1-Y still isn't to safe but if Id be him my hearing would get worse evey time I went up there.

I got that letter from Grandma and I am going to take her up on that dinner.

I'd feel a little ashimd of you if you did act like Nadine and Im proud of you for taking this in strib. Keep your head high and your eyes dry and bye god you will find that time will go one hell of a lot faster than it will if we feel sorry for our self. Besides that I'm proud to be defending my Country and our way of life. (Sound like Larry now)

I got away from that Dam Machine gun that thing is like trying to carring a rail road tie through the jungle and we had to carry 2000 rounds and man that's a lot of weight on top of the rest of our gear. So now Im a rifle man. That's what I was traind the most for anyway.

Yes we have been out on lots or portoles and the jungle in some places is so dam thick that you can't even fall down and that's the truth. Some of the fileds has grass that is over your head and is just as thick as it can be. You have to step kinda to one side to when walking through it to keep your feet from getting tangled up in the grass that has died and fell on the ground.

No there aren't a lot of Booby traps inless you get in a area where the V. C. know your coming and then there are a quit a few. Most of them you can see if you watch and man I've got good eyes.

We have had sniper fire a few times out on porthole but we haven't had any casaties by bullets yet. Some booby traps but not many in our company.

The reason so many of our boys got hurt right off hand was because one porthole thought the other one was V. C. because the other Portole wasn't suspose to even be around there but luckly the stoped it in about 5 min. but 6 or7 alreadyy got hit. None killed. But its realy not realy to bad yet. We can have good clod tea at supper and shen were at base camp like now we have moves, beer and pop. And some of these fools even go after these slant eyed women but not me my woman is in the U. S. and besides that V.D. is realy something else over here.

Well tell Linda I was glad to here from her.

You all be good and stayfit
Yours Truly
Tom or Andy
As avey one calls me here.

Tommy Capps, Investigator for Missouri State Technical
Assistance Team who worked on investigations of
crimes against children

# Chapter Eight
## Volunteers and Vigilantes

Word again traveled fast within the Mennonite community. Another assault on yet another girl, but this time the perpetrator had chosen an older girl who was able to give a detailed description. The perpetrator also knew the family was camping close by at a creek that ran through their property, and he knew that Psalm was home alone.

Psalm worked with a forensic artist, and soon we had a picture to pass among the Dutch families.

It wasn't long until a vigilante "Dutch watch" had been formed. Young Mennonite men began patrolling the gravel roads on bicycles and on foot during the ensuing nights. It was reported to me that they were carrying pitchforks and baseball bats. I met with them one evening at the Mennonite auction barn and warned them that I had better not hear that they had found the culprit and hung him from the closest tree. They all laughed at the statement, but I knew it wasn't in their character. Nevertheless, a rebel exists in all of us.

The Mennonite "neighborhood watch" men had taken their places in random ditches and gullies all along roads leading to each victim's home. Their goal was to catch the culprit who had infiltrated their virtuous lives. It was a dark, cool moonless night when a stranger appeared in the distance, slowly walking down the gravel lane toward the group of men stationed near the home of Psalm's grandparents.

Dressed in black, he epitomized Lucifer in the flesh. The three Mennonite boys sat motionless in their gully, as the figure grew nearer and nearer. Could this possibly be the man who had violated their girls?

Directly upon reaching them, they told me that one boy rustled a pile of leaves, directing the culprit's attention toward the vigilantes, and the chase was on. All three boys, baseball bats in hand, sprung up out of the ditch and gave chase, closing in on the heels of the stranger.

Suddenly, the brazen offender stopped dead in his tracks, swung around and with the cry of a banshee, he ran straight at the Mennonite boys.

They in turn, having lost their nerve, turned tail and sprinted as fast as possible in the opposite direction, but only briefly. One Mennonite boy stopped and turned to face his adversary; the other two, in staggered positions, stopped and turned just in time to see *him* disappear around a bend in the road. Being scared is nothing to be ashamed of.

One particular night two new replacements accompanied our squad on their first ambush patrol. It was a typical Nam black-as-pitch night—you could barely see your hand in front of your face.

Two soldiers accompanied me as we positioned ourselves facing the opposite direction about thirty to forty feet behind the rest of the squad, as they lay silently waiting in a ditch beside another seemingly endless jungle path. We were the rear guard—the eyes and ears preventing the ambush patrol from being ambushed by the enemy.

The next morning the "old-timers" recounted the previous night's incident. One seasoned, foul-mouthed, four months in soldier, gave a smirk of disgust as he shook his head and told the story.

"Some gooks came walking up the path right in front of the newbie's position. Then two gooks making up the rear stopped and took a piss on their heads." He got a big kick out of humiliating the pair. "They finished their business and *didi mau* on out. These two greenhorn pukes laid until daybreak in not only the enemy's piss, but their own! Fuckin' pussies; they were so scared that they shit themselves too."

I am surprised that the Mennonite boys admitted they had chickened out. I told them there was no shame in retreat. After all, what if the bad guy had had a gun?

The next morning tire and shoe tracks were found just beyond the bend where someone had pulled a car over onto the right-of-way adjacent to a fence. Casts were made of the tire and shoe impressions, but finding a match would be like finding the proverbial needle in a haystack.

~⬦~

Growing up, Jimmy and I spent a lot of time at my Poppy Whittle's home. He was a God-fearing man; however, he never talked too much religion. Grandma Whittle on the other hand was a "Holy Roller" and a strict follower of "the old time religion." Grandma knew for certain nonbelievers were going straight to hell! She told us about Jesus and the eternal fires of hell prophesized in Revelations; this dire prediction of burning forever scared me to death.

Jimmy, concerned about our fate, asked her, "What about us little kids that don't know no better?" She reassured us that Jesus took into consideration the age of a child. Still worried, I inquired about our dogs to which Grandma relieved our anxiety, "Jesus has a special Heaven for all his creatures." Grandparents have a way of making the world right.

As young boys, my brother Jimmy and I loved to walk up to the Ivy Bend Road. It was a well-worn rough and potholed gravel road that resembled the mortared roads in Vietnam. We would lay in wait, hiding in the ditches, and when a car approached, we would take turns blowing an old trumpet our uncle

Sid Luvin had given us. We would blow that horn as loud and as long as we could. This would cause a sudden braking of the passing car, and usually in a cloud of dust, the driver would jump out and look around bewildered.

One old man jumped out and hollered to his wife, "Martha, did ya' har that there horn blow? Do ya thank God jes blew the final trumpet?" Scratching his head and straining his neck as if to see if he could possibly hear another horn blow, he shrugged his shoulders and slowly climbed back behind the car's steering wheel.

As the old man and his wife drove down the road, we rolled with laughter imagining ourselves to be quite the pranksters in convincing an old man of the prophecy of the rapture! It was a lifetime and a foreign world away when I found myself in another ditch.

<hr>

Two other PFC's and I were assigned to a listening post detail. We had positioned ourselves in an old irrigation ditch about a hundred yards from base camp. The irrigation ditch was four foot deep and six foot across with vegetation growing in and around it. I assumed it was pretty long and ran alongside the base camp consisting of a company of two hundred men, about the size of two football fields.

Each listening post squad carried a radio so we could contact the central post. We answered with clicks of the reply button—one click meant okay—two clicks, something was going on, and with three clicks we actually saw somebody. When things got really scary, the radio was turned off, so as not to give our position away.

It was an active night. Just after dark, the listening post on the other side of base camp reported that they could see three Viet Cong setting up a mortar. Central command ordered them to take them out. I heard the hand grenades explode and shots exchanged. That listening post was forced to move—the enemy knew their position.

Another listening post reported sighting movement in the jungle, but they had been quiet for over an hour now.

On listening post duty, usually one man stayed alert while the other two rested. I felt on edge and couldn't sleep. Soon I heard a twig break several feet up the ditch.

Now my senses came to life, and I was fully aware of our position and its surroundings. The footsteps became more and more pronounced as they headed in our direction. The other old timer with me also heard the approaching enemy soldiers. The new guy was oblivious to the sounds and gazed ahead in a daze until nudged back to reality.

I pointed up the ditch and reached down and put my bayonet onto my M-16. The two others followed my lead. We turned off the radio, knowing they were too close and could have heard our signal. We took our guns off safety, and I laid two hand grenades on my legs.

Hand grenades would not have been a wise choice. The dense overgrowth could have bounced them right back on us. The ominous footsteps came closer and closer. I turned with my gun pointed toward the oncoming attack, but as I turned, those two hand grenades slid down my legs. To my ears, the falling grenades sounded like bowling balls rolling down the gutter lane.

To our amazement, the sounds of footsteps slowly began backing away—as slow as they had come toward us.

I gestured that we needed to move; the enemy now knew our position. The greenhorn with us was absolutely scared to death. I was now two months in and already felt like a confident seasoned veteran.

We crawled out of the ditch and away from base camp. I knew that if we moved toward our base camp we would have been killed by friendly fire. The jungle before us was dark and foreboding, but had several open areas. We belly crawled toward the dark, and there we lay on the dank, vermin infested jungle floor until daybreak. Wop-wop. Wop-wop.

⫸⬥⫷

The MSHP helicopter had landed, and with a pair of binoculars I gladly climbed on board. We found numerous shoeprints in the fields and scoured the surrounding areas.

There was an old deserted and dilapidated house with a barn several miles up the road. It appeared to me that it could be a good hideout. It was obscured by brush and tree overgrowth, making the shack a promising refuge for any criminal.

The bird turned and slowly headed toward the ground. She rested on terra firma with a firm thud, sending me to more earthly transportation, while she headed back to Jefferson City. Wop-wop. Wop-wop. Lifting off, the blade music carried my mind to a time and place when I wasn't so eager to volunteer on a helicopter.

⊷⬦⊶

When I served in the Vietnam War in 1966, we were moved from location to location by Hughes UH-1 "Huey" helicopters. Sometimes as many as twenty-five helicopters transported us; it was a sight to behold. Let me emphasize, they were bullet magnets. Coming in on a landing zone, the machine gunner would open up on the surrounding bush as a preventative measure. The chopper would shake and quiver furiously.

Sometimes when a chopper was shot down, we had to land and guard the chopper and any survivors. Our job was to wait until a CH-47 Chinook helicopter came over to lift out the downed chopper. They would hover over and lower a flight engineer down to hook up the chopper. The flight engineers wasted no time in getting their job done—they didn't want to be caught up in a ground fight.

I was with a squad of twenty-five infantrymen when we were dropped down to guard a Huey that was shot down over a deserted village. We spent two days and one night in this ghost village until the Chinook finally showed up. The flight engineer hooked up the chopper and started to raise it up when all hell broke loose. Unattached tin from the village shack roofs was lifted and hurled through the air like guided guillotine missiles.

We dove for cover as the lethal tin wreaked havoc in every direction. To our amazement, as the dust settled and we all jumped to our feet, no one lost an appendage in the chaos. We were loaded up and flown to the next Huey accident that proved to leave an indelible mark on our minds.

This chopper had flown directly into the front door of a Catholic Church and stopped before exiting out the back. Thank God, there were no civilians hurt. But sadly, the church was littered with body parts of the entire flight crew. Our horrible task was picking up the pieces and parts of men and putting them in body bags. We tried as best we could to keep all the parts of one human being in one body bag. Their dog tags were given to the sergeant who kept one and placed one in the body bag.

The very next day at our base camp, after our horrific task was completed, the sergeant announced that they were looking for volunteers for helicopter gunners. Not *one* infantryman in my squad stepped forward to volunteer.

Riding in a helicopter was a dangerous, yet thrilling, experience for a sheltered young man like me. I can remember looking down at some of the barren landscapes of Vietnam and thinking, "This looks just like pictures of the moon that I have seen in *National Geographic.*" The areas that had been bombed repeatedly, and then sprayed with Agent Orange, were as desolate as the Sahara Desert and as pitted and pockmarked as the moon.

# LETTERS HOME

Oct 18 66
19:40

Hi mom and Dad and Kigs

Well things are perty good tonight except it is raning outside now. And its perty nice in here right now.

I really don't know to mush to write about avery thing is as nice as it can be but you know how nice that it is for a place like this.

There is 5 people in our squad. Two from texas one form Calif one from Wisconson and of course Missouri. We have got one gye with 59 days left. And one with 159 days left and the other has 3 months in. And me and another gye has got a month in.

But we are all good frinds and that's what counts.

Yours Truly
Tom

Dad holding Donnie, Mom holding Marshall, Tommy (middle), Roberta, Linda, Jimmy, 1953

Tommy, Roberta, Dad (back),Marshall, Donnie, Mitchell, Linda holding Terri, Jimmy (front), 1962

# LETTERS HOME

Oct 19

17:40

Hi Mom and aveybody

Hows everyone around good ole Missouri? Hows Jimmy doing with all the girls. I gess he'll be about ready to come over about the time that I get out and settled down in good ole silvian life.

Are you feeling any better yet? If not why don't you just quit that dam job.

Im just fine tonight. Its raining again tonight and boy Im realy glad to be here in a good dry tent because after you get wet about dark you stay wet and cold all night long.

We haven't got assigned to another job yet but it won't be long and we all know it too so all were doing is weating to leave. Time goes a lot faster out on the field than here. I didn't get any mail today but Im expecting some mail tomarrow.

Well you all, Im going to close to tonight. Im just fine. Ive got 325 days left. There falling away one by one but some day they will be gone and Ill be there somewhere in the States.

You all take it easy.

Yours

Tom

P. S. Tell grampa Capps I said Hi! How is he? tell Sonny to write me.

"We see thousands of these everywhere," Tommy wrote on this leaflet. The flag on the left is the South Vietnamese flag, and the flag on the right is the Viet Cong flag.

# Chapter Nine
## Snakes, Shacks and Hootches

It was raining and cold as I cautiously crossed an open field and settled down in a ditch beside the road next to the old shack. The warm fall day had turned abruptly colder with a low front now settling over central Missouri. I wish I knew how many miles of fields and bush I had walked in my military career. Out in the bush in Nam, we humped from sun up to sundown.

❖

It was a typical day of search and destroy in the bush, when we came upon an open field. Almost instantly, from the front we began to receive sniper fire. We all hit the ground, making ourselves as low a target as possible.

Air support was called in, and soon a screaming F-4 phantom attack jet began his strafing mission above us dropping his casings on us in the wake. It sounded like hail coming toward us in long loud rips as .50 caliber casings hit all around us. The snipers ceased firing and we rushed forward, only to have an infantryman fall into one of their many punji pits. Often the Viet Cong would add poisonous snakes to the pits too. Amazingly, no, *miraculously*, when that soldier fell down in that pit, he never as much as got a scrape from one of those poisonous blades. It was indeed, his lucky day!

<hr>

I kicked at some rocks and a six-foot blacksnake came slithering out of his protection, hissing at me for intruding into his comfortable dry home. The fields held the perfect buffet of mice and rats for the snakes and the creeks provide frogs and fish. While most of the Missouri snakes are nonpoisonous, there are a few to avoid.

As young boys living in the woods, we encountered copperheads often. My momma was always reminding us to keep watch for snakes and repeatedly told the story of her unfortunate young cousin.

He was walking down a path in the Ivy Bend after dark, following his parents. His family had been visiting relatives across the "holler" and they were returning home. The youngster complained to his parents that something had just bit him. It was dark and the parents were bickering back and forth completely ignoring his cries and whines. By the time they got to their home, it was too late and the poor little guy died.

<hr>

My best friend, Sonny Webb was seining up in Franklin Creek of the Lake of the Ozarks with his uncle Floyd Harvey. Seining was the method used to scoop up large amounts of a baitfish called shad. The seine was made from a twenty foot by four foot rectangular net held by poles on each end made from tree saplings.

Sonny told his uncle at the other end of the seine that a water snake just left the bank and was swimming right toward him.

Floyd Harvey replied, "Youens need pay no mind to that thar snake, them's won't bite underwater—cause thems 'ell drown."

About that time, Sonny levitated straight up out of three foot of water with that snake still clenched down on the calf of his leg.

All us country boys learned a valuable lesson that day—forever dispelling the myth of snakes not biting underwater.

⚊⬥⚊

The snakes in Vietnam were to be avoided at all costs, especially one called two-step Charlie. We were crossing a creek one day during a search and destroy mission when one of those infamous snakes slithered into the rocks by the water.

I can't recall many names from my tour of duty, but I do remember Strobe. He pulled out his machete and charged down that creek like a madman. He caught up with the serpent and hacked it into two pieces. He rejoined us with the snake's body clenched between his teeth.

A soldier by the last name of Kahill was Strobe's best friend. They were in my company, but not in my squad. Weeks later news came that Strobe had been killed trying futilely to save the life of his buddy Kahill who had been cut down by machine gun fire. Sadly, Strobe met his fate the same way.

Suddenly the glow of a flashlight from the shack interrupted my thoughts and a shadow appeared near a window.

I was about to cross the road and move closer when car headlights popped over the hill. I held my position, and to my amazement, the car turned into the overgrown driveway of the shack. Two young boys exited the car and walked toward the shack. That is when I saw *him* walking toward the boys. His face, the face of a demon, was now completely highlighted by the car's headlights. He was carrying a case of beer.

Adrenaline surged throughout my entire being. Quickly I radioed for backup, stood up and leaped from the ditch running full throttle straight toward the boys yelling, "Hands up—law enforcement!"

They must have thought they were surrounded, and to my shock and complete astonishment, obeyed my commands.

Thinking he was only in trouble for providing liquor to minors, the boy later to be identified as the "Dutch country rapist," Garrett Ratchett, blurted out defiantly, "They told me they were twenty-one and just didn't want to buy beer because they are Dutchies."

The property was actually on the Moniteau County side of the road and the Moniteau deputies responded as quickly as possible. They had received the information about the Dutch country rapist and actually had Garrett Ratchett under surveillance. The forensic drawing from the description Psalm had provided matched Garrett Ratchett to a *T*.

The total picture of the heinous crimes committed by this worm of a man was coming into focus.

Garrett Ratchett was friends with some Dutchies who in English terms had "gone wild." He would have learned some of the Dutch language from their comradery—just enough in his deviate mind to throw suspicion toward one of their own.

He immediately "lawyered up" and had alibis for each of the nights in question.

"My wife," he claimed, "will testify I was at home on the nights the rapes occurred."

Remembering an old saying, "Women and elephants never forget an injury," I had my doubts.

Each girl identified Garrett Ratchett in a lineup as their perpetrator. Ratchett was charged with eight counts of statutory rape in the first degree, along with sodomy in the first degree and burglary in the first degree. The job now lay in the hands of the Morgan County prosecuting attorney.

My investigation, and interviews, was closed. I still had work to do back at the office compiling statements and preparing the evidence for the ensuing trial. I was the man the Mennonite's trusted, and I held that in my heart with highest esteem.

I pondered for a moment on the notion that Vietnam had shaped me into the man I am today. And while the horror of war can destroy the lives of many men who fought and survived, it molded me and my future into a man who cherishes life and the career I chose. I can die satisfied knowing that I made a positive impact in the lives of many abused children.

<hr/>

I awoke with a sudden jerk; you know the state of semi-consciousness when you dream, and suddenly your muscles contract with an uncontrollable twitch. I grasped for my weapon when one of my brothers-in-arms brought me to my senses.

He grabbed my poncho, and in a rather soft monotone, told me to get a grip; nothing was popping at the moment. It was December 5, 1966, and this was the first day of my fourth month in Country. My mind craved the peace and tranquility of the hills of Morgan County, with the now bare-branched trees contrasting sharply to the evergreen of the cedars filling the crisp fresh December air with their perfume.

Instead, my eyes focused quickly on the thirteen or so soldiers in my squad, and I was abruptly snapped back to the reality of this war.

These skinny, barefooted little Charlie bastards were persistent, and I couldn't comprehend how in the hell we would ever defeat them. The jungle heat and humidity didn't dampen the birds' or the monkeys' spirits. They were all loudly expressing their desires for the new day dawning.

We had been in the bush about three days, searching and destroying. I never knew where I was, and nobody bothered to tell a lowly PFC-E3. Later on this fateful day, I would learn that I was somewhere within Phuoc Vinh Province.

We had a tank with us on this mission, which was unusual. The tank could clear the thickest jungle, but everyone, especially the enemy, could hear us for a mile. They knew where we were and usually cleared out long before we could meet up with them. We picked up our gear and headed out on patrol.

On this particular morning, we had only been on our search for about an hour when we reached a clearing with a hootch in the middle. It looked deserted, but the gunner on the tank opened up on it with his .50 caliber machine gun.

The Vietnamese would build sleeping compartments up in the attics of these hootches that were supported with four poles. The floor level was for cooking and for the family gathering together, basically a kitchen.

The Vietnamese sympathizers would help the Viet Cong prepare their punji pits. On a previous mission, a village we entered had a large covered cast iron pot sitting in the middle of the surrounding hootches. When one of our men lifted the lid, the putrefied contents of human excrement and dead rats permeated our nostrils. Sharpened punji stakes were sticking into the brew, where they were being prepared for use in the deadly pit traps.

Our usual procedure was to search the villages, then burn them to the ground, along with any surplus supplies of rice or provisions that could feed the enemy.

As I have reiterated throughout my accounts of Vietnam, I knew very few names of my combat brothers, sometimes only last names, but mostly nicknames. Life was too brief for some combat infantrymen and attachments became liabilities.

I came in as a replacement, and I knew that out in the Real World was *my* replacement. My life was just a number to those controlling the war. Survival was my goal, if not, I would be just another statistic on the nightly news, read to the U.S. families, sitting in front of their televisions, in their safe homes. I do, however, vividly remember the name of a Lt. Weekly.

Just the day before, he had told me that I was up for a promotion to Spec-4.

After the barrage of bullets riddled the hootch, Lt. Weekly motioned for me to follow him, and we entered the hootch together. My job was to search for hidden weapons, and his was to gather any intelligence papers that might have been left behind before they *didi mau* (translated "go quickly") upon hearing our approach.

The Vietnamese dug burrows underneath their hootches and then hid them with floorboards or bamboo to conceal caches of weapons. We cautiously entered the hootch, depending upon the others to cover us in case of sniper fire.

I had never done it before, but for some unknown reason on this fateful day, I hoisted my M-16 upside down so the stock of the rifle was protecting the left side of my face.

I lifted a floor plank, and the instantaneous explosion jarred my entire body blowing me and Lt. Weekly out of the hootch.

How could I ever explain the energy that encompassed being in an explosion? There was an indescribable force and power that rocked my senses. The gut-wrenching shockwave of fragmented projectiles entered my body in midair.

I was lifted up, swung through the air, briefly knocked unconscious and back in time.

I swirled back to a cold, Christmas morning when I was seven and Jimmy was five. Mom and the Ol' Man had very little money to waste on Christmas presents, so Jimmy and I got one present that we shared. And that was all we got. But indeed, it was a splendid gift, the best gift that could have been under any kid's Christmas tree.

It was a Radio Flyer red wagon. We had gotten one each Christmas for the past three years. And that was good timing because it took us about a year to tear up a wagon. I can hear his voice to this very day, the Ol' Man's most memorable quote, "You boys could tear up a brass monkey!"

We would take our red wagon into the woods and go flying down the hills, blazing new trails through the brush. We loved that red wagon and thought we had found the perfect trail to ride down one warm summer day. It wasn't by coincidence that the creek's spring was located at the bottom of the trail. The only problem with this trail was that it wasn't long enough.

The obstacle was a rusty barbwire fence that cut off the trail prematurely. As young problem solvers, we tried our best to pull, kick and tug on that old fence, but it would not budge. It was stuck tight to the old trees it had been nailed to many rusty years before.

I had a brilliant idea—"Let's go as far up on the hill as we can, get in the wagon and slam right through that fence." For a seven year old, this made perfect sense. My brother "chickened out" or possibly had more sense as a five year old, than I did. He chose to watch the spectacle.

I rode that wagon down the hill, picking up speed as I clutched the wagon tongue, anticipating the moment of impact when the barbwire would snap in two and I would sail past the fence.

Upon impact, the barbwire slid up the tongue of the wagon, catching me right in the throat and catapulting me backwards. Jimmy thought that I had cut my head half off as I clasped my neck with both hands. Blood oozed through my fingers and ran down my chest. I could barely catch my breath as we ran home where mom lay me down to examine the wound. I was crying and even at my tender age, I could tell by the look in my momma's eyes that she was scared to death.

Luckily, the barbwire had missed my main artery by less than an inch or I would have bled to death at the bottom of that hill. Momma cleaned and bandaged my wound and sent us on our way. We set out to explore our woods and create more adventures. I had survived my fool-hearted, daredevil attempt and at that moment, I felt like a conquering hero wearing my bandages as a badge of courage.

I opened my eyes and found myself face down on the jungle floor trying to catch my breath. I had always heard that when a person is dying, his whole life flashes before his eyes. Was I dying? I wasn't ready to die, but then who is ever ready? My ears rang from the concussion and the reality of the scene moved in slow motion. I knew the routine well—my band of brothers running to secure the perimeter, bullets cutting through the jungle, then silence.

I don't remember any specific pain, just a burning sensation.

I had seen a lot of death in the three long months and one day of my combat military career in Vietnam and knew what coughing up blood from the lungs meant.

I raised my body up as if I was about to do a push up. The blood streaming from my eye began to blind me. I coughed and breathed a sigh of relief when the steely flavor of blood did not hit my taste buds.

I immediately fell back to the ground. My left arm gave out and lay useless at my side. Not realizing I had a gaping wound under my left arm, I again tried to lift my body. A medic ran over to my side faster than the flies, turned me over and injected morphine into my leg. He quickly bandaged my head and eyes. He turned his attention to the gaping wound in my left arm and tried to get the bleeding under control.

Fortuitously, the butt of my upside down M-16 took most of the brunt of the explosion. A piece of hardwood attached to a weapon had saved my life.

Lt. Weekly was also blown out of the hootch and to this day I don't know what happened to him. Did he die that day or did he live only to die in another battle?

I never knew the nature of the explosion—was it a booby trap that was triggered when I lifted the floor plank? Or did someone hiding in the bush lob a hand grenade into the hootch? I guess I will go to my grave with these unanswered questions.

A chopper swooped down from the heavens, which in military terms is called a "dust-off," and medics loaded me onto the Huey. I was completely blind with both of my eyes bandaged over, but I could hear the beautiful music of a Huey.

Was I blind? Did I lose both eyes? Swiftly they lifted the stretcher I was on into the "bird." To this very day, whenever a helicopter flies over and the wop-wop, wop-wop song of the blades fills the air, I am always transported back to the jungles of Vietnam.

One of the Medevac crewmen offered me a cigarette on the ride and shaking my head no, adamantly declined, "I have never smoked and don't intend to start now." The morphine took effect, and I drifted into a pain free dream state of unconsciousness.

My next memory was waking in a MASH hospital in Saigon and looking at the clock, it was 9:15 a.m. - 5 Dec 66, and realizing that I wasn't blinded.

The doctor walked into the room, and I immediately asked, "How is my eye?"

He replied brusquely, "It's not, but you are going home. You are one lucky son of a bitch. If that piece of shrapnel that took your eye had gone an eighth of an inch farther into your head, you would be going home in a body bag."

December 5, 1966,—the last day of my tour in Vietnam. I never got that promotion, and I really didn't give a damn—I was alive!

<hr>

I could scarcely spell, read or write when I was drafted. I kept the promise I had made to myself and God in Vietnam. I did go back to Stover High School, and I received my high school diploma at the age of twenty-three.

My stupidity and lack of resolve prompted me to quit school, but the perseverance and will, learned as a combat infantryman in the jungles of Vietnam, provided the motivation for my success.

I would wager that I have been the only high school senior with one eye to drive a school bus route. I am also positive that I am on the short list of Vietnam combat soldiers that returned from war and enrolled in high school.

# LETTERS HOME

Nov 2

21:45

Hi Mom,

Well Im back at base camp for about 2 or 3 days longer then we go out on road clearing of Route 16.

Nope we weren't the ones who Ambush those Cilvions but I herd about it and those dam stupid people breaking curfue and walked into a ambush sight at night and after 1900 intell 6:00 everything on any road is free game. That's the only way we have at all to controle Commounist movement is bye stoping everything at night bye forse. Bullets is about all these Dam fools can understand.

Yes the DMZ is a hot spot for any one to be moving into but I would tell Nadine that if I were you but that's a dam bad spot for anyone espacilly if your not inftery. Charley Cong is more scared of the US ARMY than any other force over here because we don't back down and we try like hell to never lose contact with him when we do find him.

Well Ruth's ole man went to Virginia did he. Well you know any good out fit of combat sholders has to have so mush ash and trash to keep us going.

Any one around here that isn't a combat troop is considerd the Ash and trash of the Co. bye the troops that is.

No I haven't got my paper yet?? Check into it. I'd sure like for you gyes to take some pictures and send them to me. Get some around the lake to if possible. And get the whole gang together and take a group pictrure and send it to me. You know, you, Dad, kigs and Sonny if you can hold him still long enough.

Well Im going to close for tonight. I love you all I'd better close

Yours Truly

Tom

PS Tell Jim that bye god if he inlist into the Army I'll kick his ass real good for him and I can do it to.

Besides that I should be home before he reaches that stage any way no sweat I'll just break his arm or something.

# LETTERS HOME

Nov 6—66<br>12:50

Hi you all

Well hows things around the ole farm, smelly as ever I bet!

It's nice cool day to day and were sitting here in base camp again they pulled us back from the field to stand bye for the 25th who hooked up with ole Charley. We might have to go up and put smoke on his ass but if we do we can sure do it if any one can.

We were on a 15 min alert for about 1 ½

14:00

Hi again well we just had a formation and they told us that we had been took off the stand by so will probly go back to the field tomarrow. We were suspose to be gone for 15 days but we spent 1 day and a night out before they called us back in. We have had any mail for a cupple days and so far we haven't got any today but we usually don't get mail intel 1300 and 17:00 so no sweat yet. Hows everyone? I haven't heard from my wife for a cupple days the last person I heard from was you it was mailed the 31 so Im not hurten yet.

Hows Grampa Capps coming along with his cove?
You go over there and take some picture of that
diggens and send them to me.

Couries to know how that's going to look. Has he
started to work on the upper part of his frontage lots
up above the new house.

Anether thing I'd like for some one to check and
see who owns the land from Sids around to the big
bluff on the the main channel and then from the bluff
to grampa's I thank two people owns land in there?
Send there address if you can get a hold of it.

Anether thing I'd like to find out how mush Mrs
Coming would ask for the strip of land between the
Ivy Bend road and Hommer Franklin's place. Shes so
damed bone headed that it will probley be hard to
make a deal with her but I might give it a try.

Well I gess I'll quit dreaming but if a man doesn't
dream big he'll never be big!

I'm just fine! Hows everyone there!

Well I just got three letters from Sally. Im going to
close for know

love to you all
Tom

# Chapter Ten
## Trials and Tribulations

In the courtroom, all the Dutchy girls identified their perpetrator as being Garrett Ratchett. With so many witnesses and the quality of their character, I had faith in our judicial system and the common sense of jurors to get a quick conviction. Wrong!

Before the jury trial, the defense attorneys had managed to convince the judge to dismiss Counts IV, V, VI, VII and VIII. We were down to just three of the girls receiving any type of justice and closure.

After countless hours of testimony, the jury was hung. How could they not believe these girls? I had transported all the girls and their parents to every hearing. Disappointment is not an adequate term for how we all felt.

They had placed their faith and trust in an English judicial system that failed them. The judge declared a mistrial. However, the prosecution did not hesitate to refile the charges. The girls would be forced to face their perpetrator once again and endure another long, tedious inquisition.

At the second trial, the DNA evidence was disclosed, and the now ex-wife of Garett Ratchett testified—for the prosecution.

It seems that my gut feeling about wronged women was right. The Dutchy girls all testified again, and they all endured the same lengthy grillings by the defense attorneys. The second jury came back with guilty findings on all the counts.

Ratchett was headed for the Missouri Department of Corrections for eighty-nine years.

The girls this monster molested ranged in age from five to twelve. If ever there was true valor and bravery, these girls epitomized the concept. To soldier forward and face their nemesis, not once but twice, in two long grueling trials takes more than courage. They saved countless other young girls with their fearlessness. I wish there was a Medal of Valor or Purple Heart for all the children who have the determination to face their perpetrators in our judicial system.

Today the Morgan County Mennonite community thrives. Each week our local newspaper has announcements of the joyous arrivals of newborns joining five or six siblings.

They are survivors—physically, emotionally and mentally. They buy up more land, build more homes and barns, and above all, appreciate their ordinary lives.

Talking with the defense counsel some years later, I learned that in *their* perspective, the wrong man had been condemned.

During their appellate hearings, which upheld the lower court's decision, they learned that two Dutchy boys were sent to another state for rehabilitation. The attorneys considered the boys to be alleged cohorts in some of the attacks. I was reminded of an old adage quoted to me by an elderly defense attorney, "Tommy, you got to remember, no matter how thin the pancake, there are always two sides."

There have been many trials and tribulations in my lifetime. I married and divorced twice before finding the woman who made my life complete.

My wife, Teresa, and I have been married for over thirty-one years. Our trials and tribulations have been few. I can honestly say that our marriage has been the happiest years of my life—my only regret—I didn't find her sooner.

After returning from Vietnam, I was a changed man. Small problems did not concern me. I just couldn't see the justification of people focused on trivial issues. I had cheated death, and life held an adventure to seek.

In my mind, the religious of all faiths are seeking a truth and understanding that can't be explained. I have never been a zealous religious man, but I have always tried my best to be a good, virtuous, honest, hard-working man. Some men satisfy their religious hunger with daily nourishment, while some only crave sustenance during a crisis. I believe we all need an invisible guidance, to keep us on the straight and narrow. I dedicated my life to finding justice for those innocents victimized by the evil in our world. When my final Judgment Day arrives, I hope that God looks into my heart and finds that my good deeds outweigh the bad.

I was flown out of Saigon, now called Ho Chi Minh City, to a hospital in Japan and then on to Anchorage, Alaska, to refuel. From there we flew to Denver, Colorado, to Fitzsimmons Military Hospital. I called my great-aunt Edith Luvin who was the only person we knew in Stover that had a phone. Somehow she got the message to my mom who called me back.

As moms often are, she was hysterically crying, and I could hardly get one word in. Sternly I told her, "Mom, you quit that crying right now; I am alive and only lost an eye!"

⊷⬦⊶

My mother will turn ninety years old on January 25, and she still delights in telling the story of her dream on the night of my injury. She had told dad the next day, as a matter of fact, "Tommy's been hurt. I had a dream and in my dream, Dr. Hoffa came to our door to give us the news." She emphatically insisted, "Dr. Hoffa brought a yellow writing pad and there were scribbles written on the first page explaining what has happened to Tommy."

Sure enough that very next night, Dr. Hoffa arrived at their door, yellow writing pad in hand. He had run out of gas and by the time he walked three miles to a neighbor's home for help, it was pitch black. He had managed to find the grassy trail that led to the Capps' home. My brother Jimmy answered the door and hollered for mom and dad. Mom said that she nearly passed out anticipating the worse. My momma's dream had come to fruition.

The year is now 2016, the 50th year anniversary of surviving Vietnam. I will be turning seventy years old on October 19. I have lived a good life, a fulfilled life, yet I did not escape the ravages of exposure to Agent Orange.

Agent Orange is a defoliant used liberally in Vietnam to destroy the dense vegetation. The days and nights of filling a canteen from the creeks and rivers sprayed with the deadly dioxin mixed with benzene have taken their slow toll. I was diagnosed with polycythemia vera in 2005.

There are many Vietnam veterans diagnosed with this disease and many who have silently succumbed to this disease. It is not named on the Agent Orange presumptive list. After fighting an eleven-year legal battle with the Veteran's Administration, I was finally granted service connection for this blood cancer. I also suffer from two other Agent Orange presumptive diseases: ischemic heart disease and type II diabetes.

An unpublished fact—not many Vietnam combat infantrymen live to be seventy. Maybe "He" has yet another purpose for my life.

My philosophy of life: live each day happy and to the fullest as if you are going to die tomorrow, set a good example to those who look up to you, and continue to work and learn as if you are going to live forever.

**PFC Tommy Capps, December 1966**

# LAST LETTER HOME

8 Dec 66

Hi Mom and Dad and Kiggs

Just in case you haven't heard it said yet Im on my way back state side.

Don't get all excited and scared now I just got slightly wounded bye a boobee trap and I lost my left eye. Im way thankfull that's all it did and Im sure glad to be coming home. I hope to have talked to you before you get this card but if I don't, don't get all shock up Im fine no pain or anthing. I should get a discharge. Tom

**Homecoming**

# Exhibits

Tommy was awarded the Combat Infantryman Badge, which is awarded to personnel with an infantry or special forces military occupational specialty who have satisfactorily performed duty while assigned as a member of an infantry/special forces unit engaged in active ground combat.

Hi Mom,

Well I got here just fine as well I
really have here some time tomorrow but not sure
I want to write a letter and I'm so dog-gone
in the dumps I can't even write
tonight but I figure I'd better drop
a line to let you all know that I'm
just fine and that I've already process
through & we'll be leaving here as soon
as we get transportation I'll send my address
to you as soon as I get everything that should
be before the weekend anyway but who knows.

Well mom I've got to quit now tell
every one Hi for me and take care of dad.
Be sure to tell Sonny Hi. also Grandma & Grandpa
Whittle & Capps. O.K.

See you all soon 3 or 4 days at least.

P.S. Tom
USS841739.

Did You See
Sally
Before you
left

Hi Mom. well here I am in 0 it Mas the other 16 Sept.
part of the world. the weather is great
it rains half the time. the other half
its so hot you cant barely breath
hows Dad? Did he make the operation
OK? How the Kids like School
is Grandpa + Grandma still down
to the house. Hows Grandpa
Capps OK I hope is Mr +
Mrs Wilson OK! I sure hope so.
I would like for you to give
her my address super you
self her I mean then its getting
dark and Im going to have to close
pretty soon Say Hi to everyone
for me And you all take it easy.
    By the way Im living in
a tent and Im still waiting to go
to my Regular out fit which is
on a mission now but there
suppose to be getting back any
time now. So I should leave tomarow
a pretty little outfit tonight from
all the work Ive been doing.
Ill be looking for a letter from
you all so write when you
can And send Larry's address.

~ 140 ~

we more In Closing now.
I'm just fine.

Your Son
Tommy

P.S. give my address
to Sonny if he's still
at home if not send it
to him.

PFC Tommy E Copes
US55841739
COB/BN 2 6 inf.
APO San. Francisco Calif.
96345

Hi Mom, Dad, Kigs.

23 Sept 66
1900 hours

Well Here I am back at training again. I've got 6 more days left here for my final junge trying then I get to the real thing.

I wrote Lonny a letter right after I got my address and I should here from him before tomusk long.

Well any way we haven't had anything to exciting happen yet and you know I sure as hell glad to.

During the day time around here it gets so darn hot that you can't hardly do a thing then along toward dark it begans to cool off and then it rain a little while and then it's dark and it's really petty good sleeping for a few hours and I mean a few to. Starting tomorrow we're going to be putting in a lot of hours. I haven't got any mail yet.

~ 142 ~

but a cupple of the gyes home
the rest of us are patially
weyting for our mail to get
here.
    The whole damn army over
here is made up of gyes from
FORT POLK Any way I sure
know a hellof a bunch of these
gyes.
    The other night Cherly
Norris you know from fort Polk any
way he went out on
a patrol and he said that
during the night a rain
walk up on them and they
all almost died from fright.
Then a neither one of the
gyes started to take a crap
and lit a flair they had set
out as a warning. they were so nervous
that they damn near shot that
gye. Well it's getting pritty
dark and I gess I'm to
have to close now

and go mail my letters I
wrote one to Sally to.
Be sure to tell Mrs.
and Mr Wilson Hi
for me and I'll try to
write the first chance
I get. Tell everyone
I said Hi.
How is Graps & Granda
moma? What About Dads
Operation? Hows Gradpa
Capps? Has Sonny Been
drafted yet?
Well I'll right again
when I can.
I See youa in About
51¾ weeks just gessing
Tom.

Hi Everbody.

Well Are you all doing your
shar of holding down Missouri
for me I sure hope so because
man I'm comming back there
before you gys ever miss me.
Hows Everbody making it?
They have got some of our mail
screw up somewhere along the
line And well I'm sure you
people know how the Army does
things any way. Hows Dad
feeling? Is Gradma and Granpa still
at your house? Say Hi to them
for me and tell them I would
write but I'm so dam bussy
that bye the time I write to
my wife I don't have much
time left. Hows Grapa Capps?
Hows Mr. + Mrs. Wilson.
Did Sonny get Drafted yet?
Did he get Another Car?
I would write to him but
I almost know that he'll be

in the Army before he would
get my letter. Tell him if
he's still at home Hi for
me.

Its been raining almost
every night and around some
of these tents mud is about
knee deep in most places.
We have had two gyes shoot
there then selves in the foot
just to get out of here.
And both of them shot them
selves today. We had another
gye jump off a helocopter and
knock a big hole in his knee.
And another to grab a hot
M-16 barrol and burn his hand and
two other a stept on booby traps
which just took all the hide
of off one boys foot and lower leg.
Anothe other gye got about
half of his toes took off.
I think we must have set
some kind of record because

~ 146 ~

were just stop suppose to be
in a jungle school and in
5 days out of 87 men we
have had 6 eyes get hurt
bad enough to go to the hospital
and not come back.
How the kids like School?
I have got a lot of friends
who I knew from fort Polk and
two who I knew from fort
Leonard wood. When my
time goes to getting short
I may get extended 30 days
and then E.t.S. when I get
back to the states.
Although thats a long time off
to come.
Has the weather got or getting
Cooler yet? Man here it gets
up to about 95 or 100 everyday
and the humidity is about
90 or 95 And man that makes
it really hot. And unless were in
a rubber plantation we never have

Any shade of any kind neither.
And when it Raines boy it Rain
over here.
    Tell Mr. Mrs Wilson
that I'll try to write them
the first chance I get off but
from the looks of things
it'll be at least 3 days
before I can and probly
longer. Well I better close
and go to bed because
there wont be any sleeping
tomorrow night.
    goodnight

            Your alls Son
            The Solger.
            Tom

Did Jimmy — get A CAR
yet?
    HAS Pet ANd Roy got there
House STarted up yet?
TeLL Them I SAid Hi. and tell
Roy I haven't been a hero for him yet And
still a Checker — Like Hell — But I do get Scard

~ 148 ~

6 Oct 66
1600 hours

Hi mom & Kip & DAD
    well I haven't got to much time
I've got to get my duty laundry
together and send it off today
yet.
    We have been out on the field for
5 or 6 days an we've just got in last
night leaving again in the morning.
So as you probly know it
will probley be a few more
days before you here from
me again so don't get excited
if you don't get a letter for
a few days. How's everybody?
Be sure to tell grandma that
I'll write to her the first chance
I get but I'm so pushed for
time now I just haven't got time.
My job in our squad is assistant
machine gunner when were in
a permistation and night security
when we are moving. Im
proud to be in the big red one.

but you can tell dad I'm
not trying to be any hero or
anything but I haven't been scared
yet, and we have had a few incidents
but nothing big or bad.

Although I am a little more nervous
than I used to be. And everytime I
here a pop I bite the dust and
I bet Dad knows what I'm talking
about to.

Well everbody I guess this is
pretty short but I have to get
my laundry done or I will
realy be a strong ombry around
here stinking what I Ive got
on my last clean set of clothes
now.

                    Your All's Ken
                         Tom
      PS Tell grapa Capps Hi
         Hows Dad?
I know this letter is derty but forget the
diret on it, its pretty muddy around
here in some places.

OCT 16-66
17:00

Hi Everyone
        Well we are finally back
at home base so I guess I might
be able to catch up on a few letters
and maybe tell you people a few
things. First of all our home
base is here a Phone (Tike) Vinh
that is about 40 miles North west of
Saigon so you should know
just about where I am.

        I got a letter from Linda today
I was real glad to hear from
her. Has Sally come home yet
she didn't say anything about it
in my letter but I know her pretty
good so I figured that there a 50%
chance that she would probably be
there before long.

        We are suppose to get a few days
off for about a week then we
are going down South for a few days

~ 151 ~

so I may get a chance to rest a little Although we are on brigade stand bye and if anything happens we have fifteen to be called in to help.

In Sonnys letter he descibe his Car And man it Maby sound tough I think Id really like to have that thing just to speed around in.

How you'all holding up? Hows your money holding? I gess its probley getting partly cool over there now, Man its getting hotter if anything over here. It used to rain every day and night here Now it only rains about every other night but thats a plenty when your laying out in the jungle or I poncho underthe under the stars but realy after a while your get used to it I can just lay down

~ 152 ~

anywhere And sky with do sky
awful light most of the time.
Well it's about time for chow
& bye I'll close for now and
Maybe I can write more
later on that if I don't
you all take it easy and
All are we you again after
O-well we not put it that
way I'll see you before long
Love To you all
Son

P.S. The Sgt by
By the way they got me a nick
name of Indy almost everyone
call me Indy.

P S
I got out of that dry
weapon squad I moved
Am a rifle man - Not mat
any more Safe by at
last they don't try to kill
me by carrying Ammo and

Cleaning machine our Alltine
on digging a letter position
for the same thing
you'll take care
See you all
Tom

Hi Everone,

Well here I am sitting in a nice dry tent with electric lighting and a wood floor. It rained today and by goly it sure nice to be here to especily scince its raing.

I'm realy glad to here about Sonny and I hope the he'll be never has to go. Tell him he'd better write me or I'll kick his ass good when I get back.

I'ts still isn't to safe but if I'd be him my hearing would get worse oney time I went up there.

I got that letter from Grandma and I'm going to take her up on that dinner.

I'd feel a little ashmed of you if you did not like Nadine and I'm proud of you for taking this in ~~your step~~ strib. Keep your head high and eyes dry and bye gollie you'll find that time will go on well a lot faster ~~then~~ than it will if we feel sorry for our self. Besides that I'm proud to be defending my county and our way of life. (Sound like Sonny now)

I got away from that dam machine gun that thing is like trying to carring a rail road tire through the jungle and we had to carry 2000 rounds and more thats a lot of weight on top of the rest of our gear. So now I'm a rifleman. Thats what I was traid the most for anyway.

Yes we have been out on lots of portols and the jungle in some places is so dam thick that you can't ever fall down and thats the God truth. Some of the fileds has grass that is over your head and is just as thick as it can be. you have to step kinda to one side to when walking through it to keep your feet from getting tangled up in the grass that has died and fell on the ground.

No there aren't a lot of Booby traps inless you get in a area where the V.C. know your comming and then there are a quit a few. Most of them you can see if you watch and mainly got good eyes

We have had sniper fire a few times out on partole but we haven't had any Casalles by bullets yet. some booby traps but not many in our Company.

The reason so many of our boys got hurt right off hand was because on partole thought the other one was V.C. because the other Pitole wasn't suppose to even be around there but luckly they stoped it in about 5 min. but boy I already got hit. none killed. But its realy not realy to bad yet. We can have good cloot tea at supper and when were at back camp like now we have movies, beer, pop, and some of these fools even go after these slant eyed women but not me my woman is in the US and besides that V.D. is realy something else over here.

Well tell Linda I was glad to hear from her.
you all be good and stay fit
Yours Truly
Tom or ~~Tony~~ Andy
as every one calls me here.

Oct 18-66
1940

Hi mom & Dad Kys.

Well things are pretty good tonight
except that it is raining outside
now. And it's pretty nice in here
right now.

I realy don't know to just to
write about every little thing
is as nice as it can't but
you know how nice that it
for a place like this.

There is 5 people in our
squad. two from texas one
from Calif one from Wisconson And
of Course Missouri. We have
got One gye with 54 days left
One with 159 days left And the
other one has 3 months in. And
me and another gye has got a mounth
in.

but we are all good kids and
thats what Counts.

Yours Truly
Tom

~ 157 ~

Hi mom & dad & everybody

how's everyone around good
ole Missouri? How's Jimmy doing
with all the girls. I ges he'll be
About ready to come over about the
time that I get out and settle down
to good ole civilian life.
Are you feeling any better yet?
If not why don't you jist quit
that dam job.

I'm just fine tonight. Its
raining again tonight and boy
I'm really glad to be here in a good
dry tent because after you get wet
about dark you stay wet and cold
all night long.

We haven't got assined to another
job yet but it wont be long and
we all know it too so all
were doing is weating to leave.
Time goes a lot faster out in the
field else where. I didn't get any
mail today but I'm expecting

some mail tomorrow.

Well you all, I'm going to close for tonight.

I'm just fine.

I've got ~~325~~ 325 days left - they're falling away one by one but some day they will be gone and I'll be in there some where in the States.

You all take it easy.

Yours
Tom

P.S. Tell grampa Capps I said hi! How is he?

Tell Sonny to write me.

Nov-2
21:45

Hi mom

Well I'm back at base Camp for about 2 or 3 days
longer then then we go out on road Clearing of Rout 16.

Nope we weren't the ones who Ambush these Celvion
but I herd about it and these dam stupid people were
breaking Curfiel and walked into a Ambush sight
at might and after 1900 intell o 600 everything on
any road is free game. Thats the only way
we have at all to Controle Communist, movement
is bye stoping everything at might bye force
Bullets is about all these Dam fools Can
understand.

Yes the D.M.S is a hot spot for Any
one to be moving into but I would tell
Nadine that if I were you but thats a
dam bad spot for Anyone especilly if your
not infery. Charley Cong is more scared
of the US ARMY than any other force
over here because we don't back down
and we try like hell to never lose Contact
with him when we do find him.

Well Routh's ole man went to Virgenia
did he... Well you know every good out
fit of Combat sholders has to have so much
ash and trash to keep us going.
Ony one around here that En & A Combat troop
is considered the Ash and trash of the Co.

~ 160 ~

bye the troops that is.

DO I have ~ got my paper yet?? Check into it.

Mean while Sally is there I'd sure like for you guys to take some pictures and send them to me. Get some beyond the lake to if possible. And get the whole gang together & take a group picture and send it to me to you know you, Dad, Lisa, Sally and Sonny if you can hold him still long enough.

Well I'm going to close for tonight tell my Wife hi for me and I love her. — I love you all but I love her as I have no other and there different kinds of love.

I'd better Close
Yours Truly Tom

PS Tell Jim that bye god if he enlist into the Army I'll kick his ass real god for him and I can do it to.

~~Besi~~ Beside that I should be home before he reaches that stage any way no sweat I'll just break his arm or something.

Nov-6-66
12:50

Hi you all
    Well hows things around the ole farm, smelly's
ever I bet!
    Its a nice cool day to day and were sitting
here in fase camp again they pulled us
back from the field to stand bye for the
25th who locked up with ole Charley. we
might have to go up and put smoke on his
ass but if we do we can sure do it
if any one can.
    We were on a 15 min alert for about 1½ hr

14:10
Hi again well we just had a formation and they told
us that we had ben took off the stand by so
will probly go back to the field tomorrow.
we were suppose to be gone for 15 days but
we spent 1 day and a night out before they
called us back in. we have had any
mail for a cupple days and so far we
haven't got any today but we usualy don't
get mail intell 1300 and 17:00 so no sweat
yet.
    Hows everyone? is Sally babe still there?
I haven't heard from her for a cupple days
the last person I heard from was you
it was mailed the 31 so so no sweat
yet.

~ 162 ~

2

How's Grampa Capps comming along with his
cell? You go over there and take some picture
of that diggers and send them to me
Kenny to know how thats going to look

Has he started to work on the upper
part of his frontage lots up above the new
house.

Another thing I'd like for some one to check
and see who owns the land from side around
to the big bluff on the main channel and
then from the bluff to grampa's Island two
people owns land in there? Send there address
if you can get ahold of it.

Another thing I'd like to find out how much
Mrs Comming would ask for the strip of land
between the Ive Bend road and Hammer
Trinkle's place. She is so dared bone headed that
it will probley be hard to make a deal with
her but I might give it a try.

Well I gess I'll quit dreaming but if a man
doesn't dream big he'll never be big!

I'm just fine! How's everyone there!

Well I just gote three letters from Sally
I'm going to close for know love
to you all
Tom

NOV-26-66
6:30 PM

Hi Grandma & Granpa

I was realy glad to get a letter
from you gys and by golly
Im proud to have Grandparent
that will write because you know
Im about the only one who has
Grandparent that writes.
How's Melvon? How's Beula?
Has the ole Cat tryed to drope her
litter off on you yet? Granda don't
you take them from her.
Well Im jest fine it sure
is hot over here I haven't heard from
Tony lately but it's my turn to
write to him so I can't gripe about
that part of it Can I.
I've been to Church about 3
time in the last 1½ weeks.
Well granda & Granpa
its getting dark so Im
going to close this letter
off. Be carful and you
two stay sober and don't
fight to musch Ha, Ha
Love Tom

~ 164 ~

Hi Mom & Dad and Higgs
just in case you haven't
heard it said yet I am on
my way back state side.
Don't get all excited
and scared now I just
got slightly wounded
by a booby trap
and I lost my left
eye. I'm very thankful
that's all it did and
I'm sure glad to be
comming home. I hope
to have talked to you
before you get this card
but if I don't don't go
all shook up I'm fine no pain or anything
so long for now with discharge Tom

Wishing you
the deepest joys
of the
Christmas Season
and
lasting happiness

THOSE RECEIVING THE PURPLE HEART ARE (l-r): PFC Ivan B. Boyer, PFC Tommy R. Capps, PFC Steve D. Case, PFC Vincent Croney, PFC Larry K. Pritchard, and PFC Dayle C. Schmidt. SSG Francis C. Baxter, SSG Dan H. Herbuy, SSG Abraham Hodgers, SGT Raynaldo F. Sandoval, SP 5 James C. Goslin, and SP 4 Clyde M. Canida, Jr., are not pictured.

"PFC Tommy R. Capps received a Purple Heart for wounds to his left arm and face, sustained while on a search and destroy mission near Phouc Vinh in December, 1966. He resides in Stover, Missouri."
—December 1966, *The Stethoscope*, Fitzsimmons Hospital, Denver, Colorado

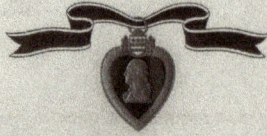

# THE UNITED STATES OF AMERICA

TO ALL WHO SHALL SEE THESE PRESENTS, GREETING:

THIS IS TO CERTIFY THAT
THE PRESIDENT OF THE UNITED STATES OF AMERICA
HAS AWARDED THE

## PURPLE HEART

ESTABLISHED BY GENERAL GEORGE WASHINGTON
AT NEWBURGH, NEW YORK, AUGUST 7, 1782
TO

PRIVATE FIRST CLASS TOMMY R. CAPPS, US55641759, UNITED STATES ARMY
COMPANY B, 1ST BATTALION, 26TH INFANTRY
1ST INFANTRY DIVISION

### FOR WOUNDS RECEIVED
### IN ACTION

5 DECEMBER 1966
REPUBLIC OF VIETNAM

GIVEN UNDER MY HAND IN THE CITY OF WASHINGTON
THIS    SIXTH    DAY OF    DECEMBER    1966

W. E. DePUY
Major General, USA
Commanding

SECRETARY OF THE ARMY

GENERAL ORDERS                                                    2 March 1967
NUMBER    1337

### AWARD OF THE ARMY COMMENDATION MEDAL

1. TC 320.  The following AWARD is announced.

CAPPS, TOMMY R  US55841739 PRIVATE FIRST CLASS E3 United States Army
Company B 1st Battalion 26th Infantry

| | |
|---|---|
| Awarded: | Army Commendation Medal with "V" device |
| Date of action: | 21 November 1966 |
| Theater: | Republic of Vietnam |
| Reason: | For heroism:  On this date, Private First Class Capps was a member of an ambush patrol near Dau Tieng.  As they reached the pre-selected site, he carefully chose a position that would afford him a clear field of fire onto a crossroad.  After waiting patiently for nearly three hours in total darkness, Private First Class Capps heard slow and deliberate steps in the dry underbrush on the other side of the road.  Two figures passed the intersection.  Private First Class Capps, being familiar with Viet Cong patrol maneuvers, held his fire in the belief that the two insurgents were the point element of a large guerrilla force. Moments later the main hostile force approached the ambush site.  With devastating effectiveness, Private First Class Capps directed an intense barrage of fire upon the insurgent force.  Numerous Viet Cong were killed in the initial barrage and the remainder retreated to regroup.  Although realizing that the insurgent survivors had not left the immediate area, Private First Class Capps, with complete disregard for his personal safety, advanced forward to search the bodies.  He was suddenly subjected to intense sniper fire.  Private First Class Capps delivered a rapid burst of fire from his weapon that silenced the sniper fire.  He then searched the bodies and recovered numerous weapons and documents.  Private First Class Capps' intrepid actions are in keeping with the finest traditions of the military service and reflect great credit upon himself, the 1st Infantry Division and the United States Army. |
| Authority: | By direction of the Secretary of the Army, under the provisions of AR 672-5-1. |

FOR THE COMMANDER:


OFFICIAL:                                           EDWARD B. KITCHENS, JR
                                                    Colonel, GS
                                                    Chief of Staff


HOWARD M. REGAN
First Lieutenant, Infantry
Acting Assistant Adjutant General

HEADQUARTERS
1ST BATTALION, 26TH INFANTRY
APO SAN FRANCISCO, CALIFORNIA 96345


'BATTLE GROUND OF TWO DECADES'


As a "Blue Spader", a member of one of America' proudest fighting battalions, you are well acquainted with the map on the reverse side of this paper. A few months ago, they were just foreign names you read about in the newspapers. Now these are places written large in the annals of the 26th Infantry, and in your memory.

But why?  Why are you here fighting in a Vietnamese war?

The Vietnamese have battled valiantly and successfully against Communist aggression for more than two decades.  But the Hanoi regime has persisted with economic and military aid in attempting to force communist rule on this tiny nation.  This economic and military aggression has put the South Vietnamese people at a tremendous disadvantage.  In desperation, they have appealed to the United States, as a member of the South East Asia Treaty Organization, and as a powerful friend, to intervene.

At first, the U.S sent economic and limited military aid, mostly in the form of Army Advisors to the ARVN (Army of the Republic of Vietnam).  Later, our government realized that in order to curb the Communist aggression in Vietnam, a large, well equipped, highly mobile fighting force was needed.  This was supplied beginning with the arrival of the 1st Infantry Division in South Vietnam in 1965.

The attempted communist take-over is a major test for the Chinese Communist principle of armed aggression.  If it fails in Vietnam, it may prove to other nations of the Communist block that armed aggression against a neighbor is futile.  As importantly, Vietnam -- this land, these people -- can with our help become a redoubt of democratic freedom and human dignity in South East Asia.

It is therefore imperative that the U.S. live up to its commitment, and render all the assistance possible to South Vietnam.  We can not falter in discouragement if the war proves long and costly -- it is likely to be so, fighting a skillful enemy through the jungles.  Nor must we lose patience with our Vietnamese allies if, depleted by two decades of combat, their forces do not resemble ours in leadership or aggressiveness.

Harsh treatment of Vietnamese, the use of insulting names such as "gook" in referring to them, and carelessness with Vietnamese property weakens them, harms our common cause, and postpones our mutual triumph. Rather, our persistant tolerance and understanding will help rebuild their strength, hasten the day when they will know victory -- and the 1st Division can leave Vietnam for service to Freedom elsewhere.

FOR THE COMMANDER:

KENNETH V. BRESLEY
Captain, Infantry
Adjutant

**Blue Spader Map at the beginning of Chapter 1**

# STATE OF MISSOURI

This certificate is awarded to

## Tommy R. Capps

in recognition of 13 years of service
to the Department of Social Services
and the State Technical Assistance
Team on the occasion of his
retirement.

_____
Ronald J. Levy
Department Director

_____
Brian D. Kinkade
Deputy Department Director

*September 2010*

# FACTS ABOUT
# THE VIETNAM WALL

There are 58,267 names on the Wall.
39,996 were just 22 or younger.
8,283 were 19.  33,103 were 18.
12 were 17 years old.
5 soldiers were 16.
There are 3 sets of fathers and sons.
31 sets of parents lost 2 of their sons.
997 were killed their first day.
1,448 were killed on their last day.
8 women are on the Wall—Nurses.
244 Soldiers were awarded the Medal of Honor
during the war
and 153 of them are on the Wall.

Following the Paris Peace Accords of 27 January 1973, all American combat troops were withdrawn by 29 March 1973. In December 1974, North Vietnam captured the province of Phuoc Long and started a full-scale offensive, culminating in the Fall of Saigon on 30 April 1975. South Vietnam was briefly ruled by a provisional government while under military occupation by North Vietnam. On 2 July 1976, North and South Vietnam were merged to form the Socialist Republic of Vietnam. The war left Vietnam devastated, with the total death toll standing at between 800,000 and 3.1 million

# Tommy Ray Capps

Tommy Ray Capps was born in Stover, Missouri, on October 19, 1946, to Robert and Lula (Whittle) Capps. He grew up in the hills of southern Morgan County and attended Proctor Grade School and the Morgan County R-I Elementary and High schools. Tommy graduated from Stover high school in 1969 after serving in Vietnam and returning home with a medical retirement due to combat injuries.

Tommy served in the United States Army, Company B, 1st Battalion, 26th Infantry, 1st Infantry Division. He was the recipient of the Purple Heart, the Army Commendation Medal with "V" Device; the Republic of Vietnam Gallantry Cross with Palm Unit Citation Badge; the National Defense Service Medal; Vietnam Service Medal and the Vietnam Campaign Medal.

Tommy and Teresa Garrison Dunklee married March 2, 1985.

Tommy's career in law enforcement began as chief of police in Stover and then Russellville, Missouri. He became a Morgan County deputy sheriff in 1979, and was promoted to Morgan County sheriff's detective in 1995.

In 1998, Tommy Capps became a member of the State Technical Assistance Team for the state of Missouri. This team was a premiere Missouri unit created for the sole purpose of assisting other agencies in the investigations of crimes against children. Tommy traveled from one end of the state to the other and upon retirement in 2010, he had been instrumental in the convictions of over 235 pedophiles, child abusers and child murderers.

Tommy Capps is the father of three children and three bonus children; Andrew Capps; Amy Weise; Anna Capps; Vanissa Dunklee; Dustin Dunklee and Desirae Lipp.

Today, Tommy and his wife of thirty-one years, enjoy their nine-acre Chestnut Orchard in Versailles. They enjoy fishing, gardening, raising chickens and traveling.

# About the Author

Teresa Garrison-Capps was born in Versailles, Missouri, on October 26, 1953, to J.C. and Willie Nell Campbell Garrison. She attended the Morgan County R-II schools where she graduated in 1971. Teresa attended Washburn University, Topeka, Kansas. Teresa has three children: Vanissa Dunklee, Dustin Dunklee, and Desirae Lipp. And three bonus children: Andrew Capps, Amy Weise, and Anna Capps.

She was a legal assistant for the Morgan County prosecuting attorney. While working for the prosecutor, Teresa met Tommy, a recently divorced deputy sheriff. They were married March 2, 1985, and blended two families.

While working and caring for a family that had doubled, Teresa attended William Woods College, Fulton, Missouri, furthering her education in Legal Studies. In 1987, Teresa was offered a position as an income maintenance caseworker for the Division of Family Services. She worked with families in crisis in eligibility determinations for Food Stamps, Aid for Dependent Children, Medicaid for the disabled and Medicaid for the elderly in nursing homes.

Teresa was diagnosed with severe rheumatoid arthritis at the age of thirty-seven and retired in 1993. Because Tommy is retired military and eligible for TRICARE, Teresa received the first of the biological drugs created for RA in 1999. These miraculous treatments allowed Teresa to complete her Bachelor's Degree in Psychology in 2002 from Columbia College.

Teresa served on the Versailles City Council from 1998 — 2002. In 2002, she also ran unsuccessfully for Democratic State Representative of the 116th District on the platform of Health Care Reform.

The biological drugs stopped the progression of joint deformities and enabled Teresa to once again dress herself, drive a car and walk. She returned to full time employment with The Missouri Department of Social Services Children's Division in 2003. During her employment with Children's Division, she worked as an investigator, alternative care worker and family centered services worker. Teresa ended her last six years of social work as the Foster/Adopt Licensing Caseworker for Miller, Morgan and Moniteau Counties, retiring in December 2010.

Teresa is pianist for the Westminster Presbyterian Church, and enjoys cooking, crocheting and making quilts.

Today, Tommy and Teresa, labor with love, on their nine-acre Chestnut Orchard, raising chickens, fishing, gardening and traveling. They also enjoy the joy, liveliness and energy their children, grand-children and great-grandchildren bring to their lives.

**Our Wedding Day**

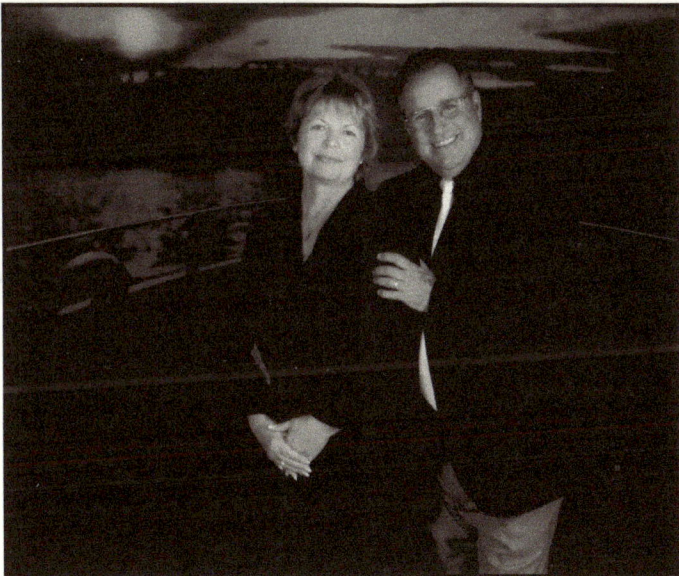

**Teresa and Tommy Capps**
**on one of their many cruises**

*The Beginning*

www.ingramcontent.com/pod-product-compliance
Lightning Source LLC
Chambersburg PA
CBHW031939090426
42811CB00002B/233

* 9 7 8 0 9 9 0 3 2 7 0 4 2 *